Sunset

ideas for great
BACKYARD
COTTAGES

By Cynthia Bix and
the Editors of Sunset Books

Sunset Books ■ Menlo Park, California

Sunset Books

vice president, general manager:
Richard A. Smeby

vice president, editorial director:
Bob Doyle

production director:
Lory Day

director operations:
Rosann Sutherland

art director:
Vasken Guiragossian

Staff for this book:

developmental editor:
Linda J. Selden

copy editor:
Phyllis Elving

photo director/stylist:
JoAnn Masaoka Van Atta

design:
Barbara Vick

page layout:
Kathy Avanzino Barone
Susan Bryant Caron

illustrator:
Beverley Bozarth Colgan

principal photographer:
Jamie Hadley

prepress coordinator:
Eligio Hernandez

proofreader:
Mary Roybal

10 9
First printing June 2002
*Copyright © 2002 Sunset Publishing Corporation,
Menlo Park, CA 94025. First edition. All rights reserved,
including the right of reproduction in whole or in part
in any form.*

ISBN 0-376-01048-7
Library of Congress Control Number: 2001094594
Printed in the United States of America.

*For additional copies of Ideas for Great Backyard Cottages
or any other Sunset book, see our web site at
www.sunsetbooks.com or call 1-800-526-5111.*

*Cover: As evening descends over the garden, vine-framed cottage
windows beckon with a welcoming glow; for another view of this
cottage, see page 32. Architect: Lee H. Skolnick. Cover design by
Vasken Guiragossian. Photography by Jamie Hadley. Photo direction
by JoAnn Masaoka Van Atta.*

Sweet retreats

This new addition to Sunset's "Ideas for Great …" series addresses a favorite fantasy for many of us—the idea of a little cottage, tucked into a back garden, that's a special retreat for writing, entertaining, potting plants, or just plain dreaming and relaxing. In these pages you'll find inspiring examples aplenty. Photos illustrate a wide variety of cottages, from rustic one-room reading shelters to beautifully appointed multiroom guest houses. Text and drawings provide down-to-earth information to help you initiate and carry through the process of planning, designing, and building your own backyard retreat.

Many professionals, manufacturers, and homeowners shared their expertise with us or allowed us to photograph their cottages. We'd especially like to thank architect Karl Golden of Berkeley, California, for his invaluable advice and ideas. For assisting with location photography in the Northeast, we thank Keiko Takayama. Our thanks also go to the San Francisco Decorator Showcase 2001; Roger Reynolds Nursery & Carriage Shop of Menlo Park, California; and Jim and Cherylyn McCalligan.

For the names of architects and designers whose work is featured in photographs, turn to pages 126–127.

contents

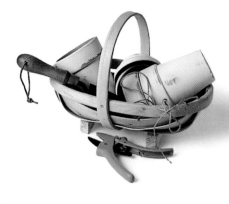

cottage
pleasures

IMAGINE AN INTIMATE SPACE, beautifully furnished and outfitted with all your favorite things, where
you can go to read, work, putter, sketch, drink tea with a
friend, or even take a long, uninterrupted snooze. The
beauties of the garden—leaves fluttering in the breeze,
warm sunshine, birdsong—are all around you.

Now picture that room or space out in your backyard, completely
separate from the house. Perhaps it's a one-room hideaway tucked in among
the garden foliage, or a bathhouse poised at the edge of a pool, or a dining
pavilion set in an expanse of lawn. Such a retreat offers one of life's great
delights—the opportunity to enjoy private time, to play, or to entertain
your friends in a setting apart from the everyday. It's almost like being on
vacation in your own backyard.

Small buildings separate from the main house are a venerable architectural tradition. From the timbered
"secret houses" of Elizabethan
England to the elegant teahouses
of classical Japan, from Victorian
summerhouses to enclosed gaze-
bos alongside Dutch canals, such
buildings have provided places
for contemplation, entertainment,
and ceremony for centuries.

For most people, the word
"cottage" conjures up a compel-
ling picture. Cottages are the stuff
of fairy tales and country villages,
of seaside, lake, and woodland—
unassuming structures tucked
cozily into their surroundings.

Cottages are where generations have dwelt in modest comfort and where, today, people go to leave behind the cares (and often the pretensions) of modern living.

Today, the style we call "cottage" is defined as much by mood as by architecture. Contemporary backyard buildings display a wide variety of forms and serve many functions. A playhouse may look like a little log cabin or an antebellum mansion in miniature. A guest house could be anything from a storybook cottage to a tent cabin. Perhaps your dream potting shed is a small version of a Victorian glass house, or your ideal dining space is an ornate pavilion in the style of an ancient Greek temple. Your cottage can be a unique expression of your own highly individual taste and your most cherished dreams.

The first section of this book, "Planning Your Cottage," introduces you to practical concerns involved in realizing your dreams. For a tantalizing look at an array of design possibilities, turn to "A Gallery of Cottages," beginning on page 33. Finally, for an overview of essential cottage components, see "Cottage Elements" on pages 99–125. Read, absorb, dream, and—begin!

PLANNING YOUR COTTAGE

BE IT A RUSTIC POTTING SHED or a gingerbread-trimmed guest house, a pool house or a home office, a backyard cottage has irresistible charm for many of us because it embodies our dream of a place that's truly our own. This chapter is designed to help you make that dream a reality—guiding you along the journey that leads from your first impressionistic visions to an actual finished cottage in your backyard. **YOU'LL BEGIN** by thinking about how you want to use your cottage and by taking a comprehensive look at your property—your main house as well as your neighbor's, your yard, and your street. Next, we take you through the steps involved in working with your local planning and building departments, in seeking help from professionals, and in considering feasibility and costs. **FINALLY,** you'll get a short course in the most exciting and creative aspect of planning your cottage: developing its style and design, both inside and out.

making basic decisions

DECIDING HOW *your cottage will be used is the starting point for nearly all of the choices you'll need to make about siting, structure, design—every aspect of your backyard addition. This is the fun part of the project, when you visualize yourself, your family, and friends using and enjoying your new space.*

How will you use it?

A charmingly civilized garden shed is a pleasant retreat as well as a practical place for potting plants and arranging flowers.

When you dream about your cottage, what do you envision? If you're an avid reader, it may be a tranquil garden hideaway open to gentle breezes. For a painter or a quilter, it's likely to be a colorful, light-filled space with tools and materials close at hand—a place where work can go on uninterrupted without ever having to be stashed away at five o'clock. For a busy working parent, it's an office that provides needed separation from the concerns of the main house; for someone else, it's a gathering place for friends and neighbors amid the beauties of the garden.

As you'll see in more detail later in this chapter, the use you'll make of your cottage will affect everything from its design details to the building regulations that govern its construction. Here are just a few possible ways you might want to use your backyard cottage:

- Mini-retreat
- Guest quarters
- Entertaining/dining space
- Children's playhouse
- Home office
- Arts and crafts studio
- Woodshop
- Potting or tool shed
- Pool house

Of course, you may put a backyard building to more than one use. A craft studio with cupboards for supplies and works-in-progress could double as a casual guesthouse, or a prettily decorated potting shed could also be a hideaway for relaxing in a rocking chair with a good book. It's all up to you.

Where will it go?

The uses you envision for your cottage greatly affect its siting: that is, where on your property it will be placed. This is a matter of simple common sense. A potting shed should be close to garden areas; a hideaway or retreat may be best tucked away along the property edge. An entertainment pavilion benefits from proximity to the main house, while a home office might be best farther away. For more about siting, see "Part of the landscape," page 12.

A crucial aspect of siting your cottage is determining your need for utilities (electricity, gas, water, sewer, telephone). If you envision a

At the end of a garden path, a guest cottage draped with roses and wisteria nestles beneath shade trees, extending an invitation to come and stay awhile.

SAME SPACE, DIFFERENT USES

HOME OFFICE

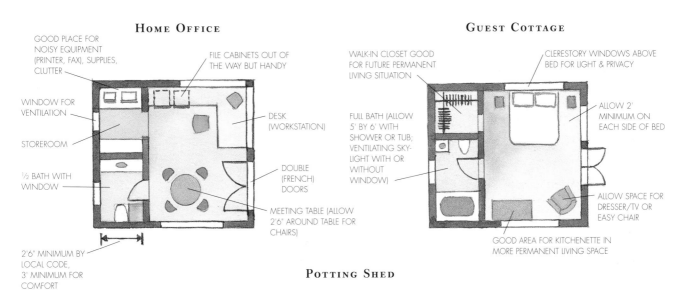

GOOD PLACE FOR NOISY EQUIPMENT (PRINTER, FAX), SUPPLIES, CLUTTER

WINDOW FOR VENTILATION

STOREROOM

½ BATH WITH WINDOW

2'6" MINIMUM BY LOCAL CODE, 3' MINIMUM FOR COMFORT

FILE CABINETS OUT OF THE WAY BUT HANDY

DESK (WORKSTATION)

DOUBLE (FRENCH) DOORS

MEETING TABLE (ALLOW 2'6" AROUND TABLE FOR CHAIRS)

GUEST COTTAGE

WALK-IN CLOSET GOOD FOR FUTURE PERMANENT LIVING SITUATION

FULL BATH (ALLOW 5' BY 6' WITH SHOWER OR TUB; VENTILATING SKYLIGHT WITH OR WITHOUT WINDOW)

CLERESTORY WINDOWS ABOVE BED FOR LIGHT & PRIVACY

ALLOW 2' MINIMUM ON EACH SIDE OF BED

ALLOW SPACE FOR DRESSER/TV OR EASY CHAIR

GOOD AREA FOR KITCHENETTE IN MORE PERMANENT LIVING SPACE

POTTING SHED

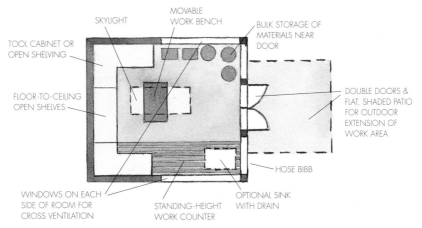

SKYLIGHT

MOVABLE WORK BENCH

BULK STORAGE OF MATERIALS NEAR DOOR

TOOL CABINET OR OPEN SHELVING

FLOOR-TO-CEILING OPEN SHELVES

DOUBLE DOORS & FLAT, SHADED PATIO FOR OUTDOOR EXTENSION OF WORK AREA

WINDOWS ON EACH SIDE OF ROOM FOR CROSS VENTILATION

STANDING-HEIGHT WORK COUNTER

OPTIONAL SINK WITH DRAIN

HOSE BIBB

Constructed with Spanish cedar siding and trim of recycled redwood, a classic cottage blends gracefully into its woodsy surroundings. Equipped with kitchenette and bath, it can function as a guesthouse or an office.

very simple space—a freestanding screened retreat, for example—in which to relax during the daytime, this probably isn't an issue. But if you want water and electricity, your plans become more complicated.

You'll want to find out right away where utility lines and pipes are located on your property and whether you can hook up to them (see page 17), and you'll need to pay a visit early in the game to your local planning/zoning department (see page 21) in order to get an idea of your project's feasibility.

How big should it be?

How much room do you need? This is a case in which "small" really is "beautiful," since much of the charm of a cottage lies in its miniaturized quality. That simple getaway space could be quite small—say, 10 by 10 feet. A guest cottage could be as small as 12 by 14 feet or as generous as 20 by 30 feet.

A tape measure is your best tool for getting a rough idea of the space you need. Go through your home, or that of a friend whose rooms you like, and take down the dimensions of various rooms. How big is a comfortable bedroom or a small playroom? How much counter or desk space does a home office require? Looking through books about remodeling specific rooms can also be helpful in determining dimensions. Don't forget that a tiny cottage can also gain a feeling of expansion with the addition of a small porch, a deck, or even a bay window.

Your tape measure will also help when you're considering the furnishings and equipment you want to include. Will you want to do yoga in your cottage? Measure the length of your yoga mat. Are you going to use the space for weaving or designing with fabrics? Measure your loom or your cutting table and sewing machine table.

Of course, storage is important, too. You'll need shelves and/or cupboards for those fabrics, that yarn, or your dishes. How many books do you want on the shelves of your reading lair? If you're planning a shed for potting and puttering, gather your tools, a typical assortment of pots, and other necessities to see how much space they take. Plan for more storage space than you think you need, if at all possible.

Looking ahead

No matter how you intend to use your cottage now, it's wise to think ahead to different ways you might use it in the future. Circumstances change: children grow up and move out, parents move in, or a home office becomes necessary. It's a good idea to make your space as flexible as possible. A children's playhouse can be made to a scale that will suit the little ones now but also accommodate a home office when the kids are grown. Conversely, your poolside cabana may be a perfect space to transform into a separate dwelling for your child-become-teenager. Your summerhouse (perhaps with some special adjustments) may make way for an elderly parent.

The elegance of this little shed belies its humble function as a storehouse for garden gear. Its handsome roof line and accompanying Chippendale-style bench make it a focal point in the carefully designed landscape.

To allow for such eventualities, it's a good idea to include utilities in your cottage from the start or make sure that they will be relatively easy to add later.

It could be a children's playhouse, but the tiny structure at right, just 6 feet across, is used as a potting shed. Inside, a potting bench holds bedding plants and gardening paraphernalia (above). A spirited color scheme—created with tung-oil stains—and decorative trim create one-of-a-kind appeal.

site specific

WHERE YOU PLACE *your cottage will be determined partly by your own desires and aesthetic leanings, partly by local regulations governing the building of any structure, and partly by the nature of the property itself. For an overview of these important considerations, read on.*

Fitted perfectly into the landscape, a handsome pavilion is a focal point at the apex of converging beds of perennials.

New or remodeled?

Will your backyard cottage be entirely new construction or a replacement or renovation of an existing outbuilding? Many properties already have a storage shed, an unused detached garage, or even an old barn. To create a livable new space out of such a building, begin by evaluating its condition, location, and good and bad points. It's a good idea to consult an architect or a contractor for a realistic evaluation.

A new structure built from the ground up on a new site usually must fulfill numerous code and zoning requirements (see pages 20–21). But an existing building that you remodel—or even a new but same-size structure on the same site as an old one—may not be subject to the same requirements. Check before proceeding.

Part of the landscape

When deciding where to place a new cottage, consider both how it will look in your landscape and what you want to see when you are inside the structure, looking out. Do you want to be able to see your cottage from the house or from particular places on your property? You might want to be able to observe a children's playhouse from your kitchen window, but you might want a potting shed or a guesthouse to be largely concealed. Privacy might be called for in a writer's space, but an area for entertaining might benefit from a closer connection with the main house and the garden at large. Also consider access; a potting shed should be near the garden areas it will serve, and a dining area should not require a long walk from your kitchen.

What was once a garage has been transformed into a dazzling poolside guest house. Zoning ordinances dictated that the original 20-by 24-foot size be maintained, but adding a windowed roof monitor and a porch was allowed—to dramatic effect.

No matter what its function, a well-designed cottage can be an attractive feature of your landscape. It can serve as a focal point, drawing your eye to an especially pretty corner of the property or distracting the eye from a not-so-attractive neighboring house. Or it can be a delightful surprise waiting to be discovered around a bend.

Wherever you place your cottage, you will want it to relate comfortably to its surroundings. Perhaps you would like it to be surrounded by trees and foliage so that it looks like an integral part of the landscape. If you can, place it where there are already mature plantings. If that's not possible, find out what fast-growing trees, shrubs, and vines would be good choices for your climate and exposure. And don't forget that flowering plants, in beds and borders or in containers and even window boxes, can add charm and color. In fact, creative landscaping

Flowering plants spilling over and around a structure are the essence of cottage charm. Allow roses to clamber up walls (below and right), or plant a window box with a generous helping of flowering plants and vines (below right).

will help ensure a graceful transition between cottage and garden that will enhance both.

To determine how to orient your cottage, look in all directions from the proposed site to get an idea of available views. You may want to look back at your house or garden from the cottage, or you may want to get a sense of complete detachment, either by partially screening the view with plants or a trellis or by tucking the structure out of sight. If you have a beautiful view toward mountains, a meadow, or a lake, you may want to look out on that. And, of course, you want a "good-neighbor" cottage, one that will not encroach on your neighbors' views, sunlight, or privacy—or be subjected to unwanted sights or sounds from next door.

Consider your climate

In addition to aesthetic considerations, think about your cottage's placement in relation to weather conditions. Is it hot much of the time where you live? Is there a high average annual rainfall? Do you live in an area with dramatic seasonal changes, or in a climate that's relatively

Tucked away at the end of a garden path, this cottage stays cool on even the warmest afternoons, thanks to abundant shade provided by surrounding trees and mature shrubs.

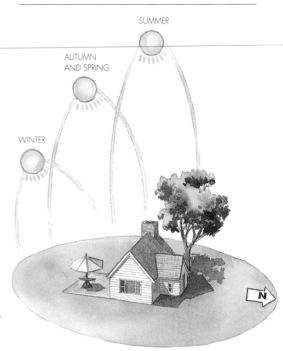

Sunlight strikes your property at predictable angles, depending on the time of year and where you live. The sun's arc is higher in summer and lower in winter.

mild year-round? These factors affect how your cottage will need to be sited.

Do you want a sunny spot or a shaded, sheltered one? In a hot climate—or on especially warm days anywhere—shade is welcome, but most spaces benefit from the sun's warmth and light at least some of the time. Still, you don't want to be trapped in a space that feels like a sauna! Sheltering trees can help, as can shutters, curtains, and nearby water— a fountain or a small pond—to cool the surrounding air. Deciduous trees, shrubs, and vines planted around a structure will afford shade in the summer and let in light and warmth in the winter, when the branches are bare.

Observe the sun's position at various times of the day and, if possible, different times of the year. Generally, a northern exposure is cool because it rarely receives sun. An exposed south-facing location is warmer because, from

sunrise to sunset, the sun never leaves it. An east-facing property is cooler, as it receives only morning sun, while a structure that faces west is often hot because it receives the full force of the sun's afternoon rays. These factors will affect where on your property you place your cottage as well as how you orient the building itself. For example, a building with south-facing windows will benefit from an overhang on that side; this will partially shade it from summer sun but let in light in winter, when the sun is lower.

Looking at practicalities

Many other practical considerations will also affect where you site your cottage. These include the configuration of the ground (is it level or sloping?), soil conditions and drainage, other structures and paved areas on your property, zoning restrictions (see page 21), established plantings and trees, and your cottage's relation-ship to neighboring houses and lots as well as to the street.

You'll also need to consider the locations of utilities—gas, electric, television cable, water, and sewer. In the simplest of scenarios, a potting shed may require water but not electricity; in that case you can either make use of a nearby hose bibb or plumb in a sink, the latter calling for some kind of drainage as well as water pipes. A home office will require electricity and tele-phone lines but not necessarily plumbing. In the most complex scenario, a fully equipped guest cabin with bath requires a sewer connection, water lines, and electrical hookups.

Seasonal use is another important considera-tion in determining what utilities you'll need. Will this be a summertime-only retreat, or an all-season one? In all but the balmiest climates, three- or four-season cottages require a heat source (see page 114).

SLOPING SITES

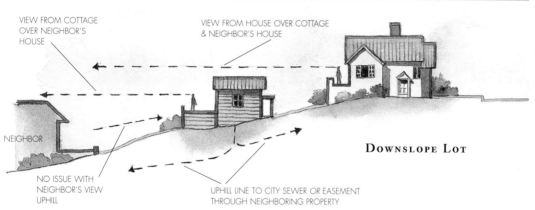

VIEW FROM COTTAGE OVER NEIGHBOR'S HOUSE

VIEW FROM HOUSE OVER COTTAGE & NEIGHBOR'S HOUSE

NEIGHBOR

NO ISSUE WITH NEIGHBOR'S VIEW UPHILL

UPHILL LINE TO CITY SEWER OR EASEMENT THROUGH NEIGHBORING PROPERTY

DOWNSLOPE LOT

On a sloping lot, you must consider such factors as water runoff and drainage, sewer lines (flowing downhill or helped uphill by means of a pump), and sight lines in relation to neighboring structures.

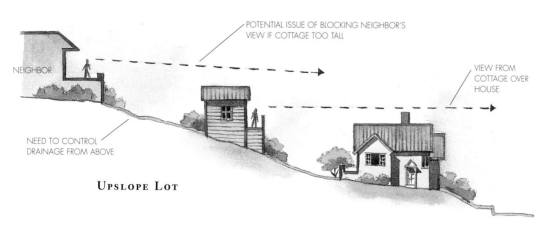

POTENTIAL ISSUE OF BLOCKING NEIGHBOR'S VIEW IF COTTAGE TOO TALL

NEIGHBOR

VIEW FROM COTTAGE OVER HOUSE

NEED TO CONTROL DRAINAGE FROM ABOVE

UPSLOPE LOT

creating
a site plan

BEGIN WITH WHAT ARCHITECTS CALL *the "broad brush" approach. The easiest, quickest way to get a general idea of where your cottage should go is to do a small-scale sketch of your property showing the relationships among its various elements—property lines, existing structures, plantings, pavings, and so forth.*

This simple drawing doesn't have to be of professional quality, but it should be neat enough and sufficiently accurate in scale to serve as a preliminary plan to show to your local planning department, your banker if necessary, and perhaps your neighbors. It will also provide a starting point for discussion if you work with an architect or designer and/or a contractor.

With the help of a partner, take rough measurements of your lot and its various features, using a tape measure at least 50 feet long. (Sometimes you can save time and effort by obtaining dimensions and gradients from your deed map, house plans, or a topographical map of your lot. Or they may be available through your city hall, county office, title company, bank, or mortgage company.)

For your rough sketch, use plain paper or a sheet of graph paper with ¼-inch squares. (A common scale for site plans is ⅛ inch = 1 foot.) At this stage, you want to keep your drawing small and simple so that you can focus on the big picture and work through a lot of ideas quickly.

The following information should appear in one form or another on the site plan. Some details, such as the locations of utilities and

easements, can be left until later if obtaining the information is problematic at this stage. However, if your property is on a slope, it's important to indicate that on this first sketch.

- **PROPERTY LINES AND DIMENSIONS.** Outline your property accurately and to scale (to within a foot or so), and write its dimensions on the site map. Note the locations of fences and walls, streets and sidewalks, property lines, and neighbors' houses. Right now all of this is still fairly inexact; you may need to obtain more precise surveys when you're further along in the planning process.

- **BUILDINGS.** Show your house and any other structures on your property, to scale. Show relevant doors or windows, such as a door that leads to where your cottage might go or a window that looks out on your backyard.

- **PAVED AREAS.** Show all driveways, paths, steps, patios, and decks.

- **EXPOSURE.** Draw an arrow to indicate north; then note shaded and sunlit areas of your landscape. Indicate the direction of the prevailing wind and note any microclimates, such as hot spots or deeply shaded areas that stay damp and cool all the time.

- **EASEMENTS.** Easements give utility companies, local municipalities, or sometimes neighbors the right to enter your property, usually to run electric lines, sewers, and so on. You usually cannot build within an easement.

- **UTILITIES.** If you're planning amenities that call for installing utilities, you'll need to map sewer, water, gas, and electric and cable television lines. You can do this now or wait until later. But keep in mind that any plumbing requires a sewer connection or a septic tank. (Sewers depend on gravity and must run downhill; otherwise they require a pump.) Utilities for a cottage will almost always be run from the main house and use the same meters.

- **GRADIENT AND DRAINAGE.** If applicable, indicate the general slope and any significant high and low points on your property. (A professional topographic survey may be required later, during the design phase.)

- **EXISTING PLANTINGS.** Note established trees, shrubs, planting beds, and borders.

- **VIEWS.** Note all views, attractive or unattractive. If appropriate, you can use a ladder to check views from different elevations. Consider how a backyard building might be viewed from inside the house, from various positions on the property, and from nearby houses or streets.

- **NEIGHBORHOOD.** Unless you live on a very large property or out in the country, you will probably find it useful to make a rough sketch of your immediate neighborhood as shown on page 18. Evaluating the positions of streets and neighboring houses will help you decide on the best location for your cottage and will also be useful to your local planning department in evaluating the site.

Trying out possibilities

Once you have drawn your plan, you can begin to play with different possible sites for your cottage and with differing configurations for the footprint, or ground floor area, of the building itself. For each scheme, place a separate sheet of

A SAMPLE SITE PLAN

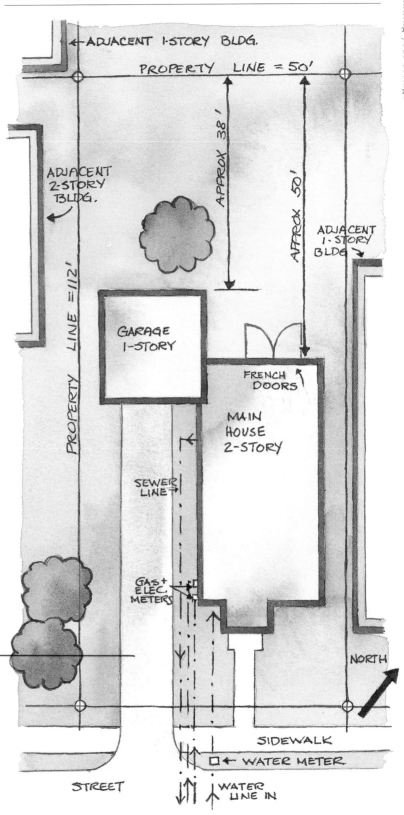

tracing paper over your site plan and sketch in a rough shape to represent the location and approximate footprint of your proposed building. Then you can study how it relates to surrounding foliage, the house, and the neighborhood. To enhance you cottage, you can experiment with paths, patios or decks, and planting areas—elements that provide a transition between cottage and garden.

There's a "flow" among areas in your yard, just as there's a certain "flow" among rooms in your house. Can you create an easy, natural pathway from the house to the cottage? Can you tuck the cottage among established trees, so that it becomes a private retreat? How can you orient cottage windows toward the sun without feeling exposed to the sight lines from your neighbor's second-story deck? Using tracing-paper overlays on your site map lets you try out many solutions to your particular issues until you come up with one that you like.

NEIGHBORHOOD PLAN

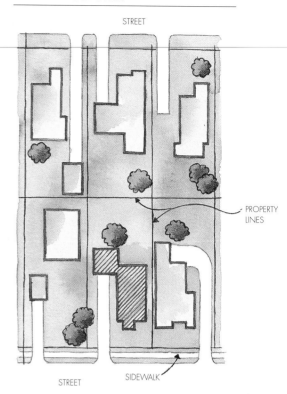

STREET

PROPERTY LINES

STREET   SIDEWALK

Set above the garage on a hillside lot, this artist's studio required special attention to foundation and drainage issues as well as its relationship to neighboring structures.

ONE SITE, THREE VARIATIONS

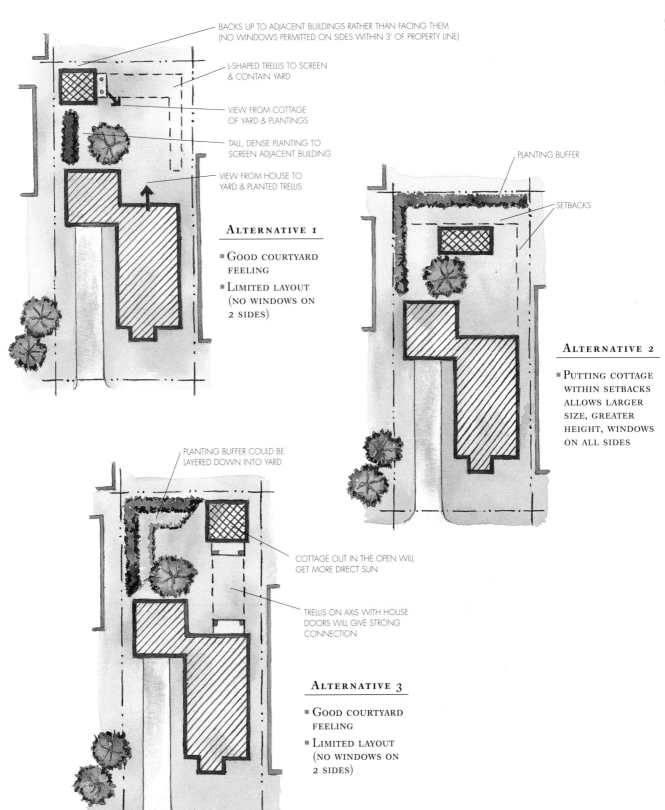

BACKS UP TO ADJACENT BUILDINGS RATHER THAN FACING THEM
(NO WINDOWS PERMITTED ON SIDES WITHIN 3' OF PROPERTY LINE)

L-SHAPED TRELLIS TO SCREEN
& CONTAIN YARD

VIEW FROM COTTAGE
OF YARD & PLANTINGS

TALL, DENSE PLANTING TO
SCREEN ADJACENT BUILDING

VIEW FROM HOUSE TO
YARD & PLANTED TRELLIS

PLANTING BUFFER

SETBACKS

ALTERNATIVE 1

- GOOD COURTYARD FEELING
- LIMITED LAYOUT (NO WINDOWS ON 2 SIDES)

ALTERNATIVE 2

- PUTTING COTTAGE WITHIN SETBACKS ALLOWS LARGER SIZE, GREATER HEIGHT, WINDOWS ON ALL SIDES

PLANTING BUFFER COULD BE
LAYERED DOWN INTO YARD

COTTAGE OUT IN THE OPEN WILL
GET MORE DIRECT SUN

TRELLIS ON AXIS WITH HOUSE
DOORS WILL GIVE STRONG
CONNECTION

ALTERNATIVE 3

- GOOD COURTYARD FEELING
- LIMITED LAYOUT (NO WINDOWS ON 2 SIDES)

getting down
to business

NOW THAT YOU *have something on paper, it's time to determine whether your project is feasible. This depends on two important factors: your budget and approval from your local planning and building departments. Below, we guide you through these crucial preliminary steps.*

Dollars and sense

This trim-looking office is just a few feet from the fenced property in a corner of the yard. By code, windows are not allowed on the two back walls.

Before you proceed too far along with your plans and dreams, it's crucial to take a cold, hard look at budget. Many planned projects never get built because of inadequate attention to this aspect of building a cottage.

For a rough idea of expenses without involving architects or contractors at this stage, use basic square-foot costs in your calculations. The square-foot figure will vary according to where you live, what utilities you want, and other factors. Call around to general contractors in your area (get names from the phone book or from friends and neighbors). Describe your site, how you plan to use your cottage, and access for building equipment and supplies. Ask what a range of square-foot costs might be for such a project, and multiply these figures by the proposed square footage of your cottage. Then you must add building and permit fees, fees for an

architect or designer if you will use one, and fees for surveys, soil reports, utility hookups, and other requirements.

Once you know what you can realistically expect, you can scale down or expand your ideas according to your own budgetary constraints. Maybe you'll decide you can paint or sculpt perfectly well in a smaller space; or maybe you'll be delighted to find that you can afford to plumb in a small sink in your potting shed.

A visit to your planning department

If you're putting up a simple garden shed on a large country lot, you can most likely go ahead with whatever site and design you choose. But in most places, you must follow specific guidelines governing construction of what's sometimes called an "accessory building."

Your site plan sketch will be your most helpful tool in determining whether your project is feasible. Begin by taking it to your local planning department officials. Usually they can tell you right away about any restrictions. These might include how many square feet your cottage can be, how far from your property line it must sit, how tall it can be, and whether you can build a structure for use as an office to which clients will come. If regulations limit your plans, you may be able to get a variance through the planning department.

You will probably need to deal with two city or county departments, each with its own set of codes or ordinances.

THE PLANNING/ZONING DEPARTMENT oversees the broad picture. Zoning regulates what building uses are allowed—commercial, industrial, or residential. (This may affect a home office, which may require client parking, for example.) The planning/zoning department determines how high your building can be, how much of your lot it can cover, and where it can be placed on the property—specifically with regard to setback, or distance from lot lines. In some circumstances, the planning department may require you to obtain a survey of your lot.

BUILDING RESTRICTIONS

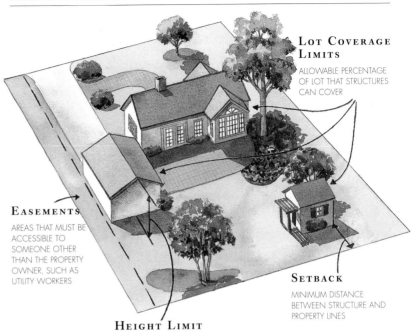

LOT COVERAGE LIMITS
ALLOWABLE PERCENTAGE OF LOT THAT STRUCTURES CAN COVER

EASEMENTS
AREAS THAT MUST BE ACCESSIBLE TO SOMEONE OTHER THAN THE PROPERTY OWNER, SUCH AS UTILITY WORKERS

SETBACK
MINIMUM DISTANCE BETWEEN STRUCTURE AND PROPERTY LINES

HEIGHT LIMIT
MAXIMUM HEIGHT FOR STRUCTURES

You may be asked to erect "story poles"—a rough framework of vertical 2 by 4s that outlines the cottage's proposed "envelope" (its three-dimensional outline) and shows whether it will block neighbors' views, shade their sunny yard areas, and so forth.

Sometimes the planning department will require a *design review* to decide if certain architectural design standards have been met. In a development community or historic neighborhood, for example, your design, site, and building details—even your choice of trees—may be subject to review by a homeowners' or historical preservation committee.

THE BUILDING DEPARTMENT is concerned with specifications for the building itself—with its safety and structural integrity. The Uniform Building Code, which is similar from place to place, sets standards for materials and construction, addressing safety issues, structural elements, utilities, sewers, and so forth. You must get a permit from this department before you can do any work. An inspector will visit the site periodically during construction and must sign off on the job when it is finished.

launching
the process

ONCE YOU'VE DONE *the preliminary legwork, it's time to get down to details. Let's assume your general idea and site for the cottage have been given preliminary approval by the planning department. This is the point at which you begin to make decisions about whether to hire professional help and how much of the work to do yourself.*

Professional help or DIY?

Deciding whether to do it yourself or to use the services of professionals should come early in the planning process, whether you're remodeling or building from the ground up. It's vital to be realistic about your skills and your available time. Building a backyard cottage is basically the same as building a house, except on a smaller scale. It may require everything from laying a foundation to framing and roofing to plumbing and electrical work.

If you are an experienced builder or designer, or if your cottage will be a simple affair on level ground, you may consider designing and building it yourself, either from "scratch" or from a kit or mail-order plan (see facing page). Or you may want to use professionals for some aspects of the project and do some parts yourself.

If you do build it yourself, you can always subcontract jobs you don't feel comfortable doing—pouring a foundation, for example, or doing the electrical work (see "Subcontractors" on page 24). Work on a detached backyard structure usually doesn't greatly disrupt daily life, so the slower pace of a weekend do-it-yourselfer isn't necessarily a problem.

Designed and built by the owner, this shed is roofed and faced with pressure-treated pine plank pieces.

If you decide to hire an architect or designer, you can expect a creative professional approach and a unique and attractive design. You'll usually save time and money by involving these professionals early in the process, probably soon after you've taken your initial site plan sketch to the city building department. Besides creating the design, an architect or designer can help you evaluate your budget realistically, deal with codes and permits, and generally move the project along through construction to completion. To learn more about the work of architects and other professionals, see page 24.

Alternative approaches

If you want an original design created especially for you, your best choice is to hire an architect or a building designer. But two other options—a kit or prefabricated structure and mail-order plans—can work well if you don't require a site-specific building design. Another option is to select a prefab or mail-order cottage or shed but get help from a builder in putting it together. You can also hire an architect to help set it artfully into your landscape or customize details.

KITS AND PREFABS. Prefabricated cottages and sheds are available in a variety of styles, from canvas-sided bungalows that you erect on site-built wooden platforms to fanciful playhouses or elegant glass summerhouses. Some can be ordered in kit form that an experienced do-it-yourselfer can put together; others require consultation with a company representative, who tailors the design to your needs, then installs the prefabricated components or works with your architect or builder to install them.

Do-it-yourself projects often offer great flexibility, because you can add your own personal touches to the basic prefabricated elements. Approaches vary with the manufacturer.

Look for advertisements for prefabricated buildings in home and design magazines, or do research on the Internet. As with any building put up on your property, you must comply with local planning and building department requirements, which will probably include filing for a building permit. Ask before you order!

MAIL-ORDER PLANS. Garden and building magazines, and some books, offer plans you can send away for. Some books include the plans themselves. Depending on your building expertise, you can use such plans to build a structure yourself or to guide a professional contractor,

On the facing page, a bold two-story structure features a striking combination of barrel and shed roofs—the work of an architect's imagination and expertise. Below, an 8-foot-square enclosed workshop with covered, lattice-screened storage area was built from mail-order plans.

planning your cottage

PROFESSIONAL PROFILES

Building professionals can help you in a variety of ways, as summarized in the following brief overview. Sometimes a range of services is offered within a single design-build firm, including the work of architects, designers, and contractors.

- **Architects.** These state-licensed professionals have a bachelor's or master's degree in architecture. When you hire an architect, you're hiring a highly trained imagination capable of creating a livable space that's beautiful as well as structurally sound. Architects' fees may be a percentage of construction costs (ranging roughly from 10% to 15%), a lump sum, an hourly rate, or a combination.

- **Building designers.** A building designer may be licensed (by the American Institute of Building Designers or, sometimes, as a contractor) or unlicensed. If you know exactly what you want, these professionals can translate your ideas directly into plans. Hiring an unlicensed building designer gives you less legal protection in the event of trouble, but his or her fees may be lower. Note that even a building designer with a contractor's license may need to subcontract to an architect or engineer for some structural details and calculations.

- **Draftpersons.** Drafters may be members of a skilled trade or unlicensed architects' apprentices. From a design done by you or your architect, they can produce working drawings (from which you or your contractor can work) needed for building permits.

- **Landscape architects and designers.** The integration of your cottage with your landscape is usually an important issue, and landscape professionals can help you create a satisfying relationship between indoors and outdoors, building and garden. Sometimes an architect or building designer will perform this function. But landscape professionals usually have a greater knowledge of plants—how to choose and install them.

- **Structural and soils engineers.** If you're planning to build on an unstable or steep lot or use an unusual structural design, you should consult an engineer. A soils engineer evaluates soil conditions and establishes design specifications for foundations. A structural engineer, often working with the calculations a soils engineer provides, designs the building structure, including foundation piers and footings to suit the site. Engineers also provide wind- and load-stress calculations as required.

- **General contractors.** Licensed general contractors specialize in construction, though some of them have design experience as well. They may do all the work themselves or hire qualified subcontractors while still assuming responsibility for ordering materials, coordinating subcontractors, and seeing that the job is completed according to contract.

- **Subcontractors.** If you act as your own general contractor, it's up to you to hire, coordinate, and supervise whatever subcontractors the job requires—such as carpenters, plumbers, and electricians. You'll be responsible for permits, insurance, and any payroll taxes. Besides doing the work according to your drawings, subcontractors can often supply you with product information and pick up materials for you.

Choosing a professional

To find an architect or designer, begin with the best source of all—personal referrals. Ask friends and neighbors for their recommendations, and look for architects' or designers' signs on job sites. You can also check with local and state chapters of professional organizations such as the AIA (American Institute of Architects).

Once you have collected a few names, interview the professionals to get a sense of what it would be like to work with them. Look at photographs or visit the sites of similar projects with which they've been involved, and talk with the homeowners. Try to find a professional with whom you can communicate easily and whose opinion and taste you trust.

Built from mail-order plans, a cooking cabana has an extra-wide opening for moving patio furniture inside for dining. The window box is the owner's personal touch.

codes, ordinances, regulations, and require-ments, including permits and inspections at the time of construction. Many cities and states now require that an architect or engineer review, stamp, and sign a plan for a large structure prior to construction. To find out if this is true in your area, contact your local building department.

Project phases

Whether you do some or all of the planning and work yourself or hire professionals all the way, the process of designing and building your cot-tage will probably follow the same basic pattern.

■ **PROGRAMMING PHASE.** This architect's phrase refers to the stage during which you and/or your architect or designer gather all basic information relevant to your project. Here's where you review your collection of clippings and photos, talk about your ideas and dreams, and collect hard data such as boundary and topo-graphical surveys, utilities information, and plan-ning department regulations. You also become

Tucked beneath the intriguing roof of this summerhouse is a stylish workspace, complete with computer. The elegant octagonal structure, built to custom specifications, was fabricated in sections and shipped to the site for assembly.

builder, or carpenter. Often, you can use a basic shed plan to construct a structure, then individ-ualize it by adding special design details.

Photographs or drawings of completed struc-tures show you their general look, although details are usually available only with the plans. In addition to specifications for the basic exteri-or structure, the architectural blueprints offered often include construction details for siding, flooring, roofing, windows, skylights, doors, and extras such as interior shelving, decorative cupo-las, and lattices.

Packages usually contain two sets of detailed plans. You'll probably need multiple sets—for obtaining bids and permits, for reference at the building site, and, if applicable, for your lender. Some subcontractors—foundation, plumbing, electrical, and HVAC (heating, ventilation, and air-conditioning)—may need partial sets.

Most mail-order plans are authorized for use on the condition that you comply with all local

planning your cottage

practical about budget, getting a clear idea of how much the project is likely to cost and what's affordable for you.

■ **DESIGN PHASE.** This is both the most challenging and the most exciting phase of your project. You and/or your architect will explore design concepts as well as siting options (based on what you've learned from your local planning department). Through a series of rough sketches, both the exterior shape and the interior design will evolve. You might want to experiment right on your proposed site with "story poles" (see page 21) to help you visualize how your proposed building relates to its surroundings.

Now is also the time to have surveys made by licensed surveyors, if that hasn't already been done and the building department requests them. One kind is a survey of your property's boundaries. The other, a topographic survey showing land contours, is important if your land isn't flat.

Of course, you will also develop the building's style and design, from the outer "skin" to each interior detail. When it all finally comes together, your architect or designer (or a drafter) will create drawings for submission to the plan-

Exterior design details such as this cottage's storybook roof and fascia help to establish a structure's character.

ning/zoning department. These may include a neighborhood plan, the site plan, floor and roof plans, and exterior elevations (see facing page). Once these are approved, final construction documents, or working drawings, can be created from them, specifying materials, products, and finishes as well as all building details. The working drawings will be submitted to the building department for a plan check and a building permit (which may take several weeks) and to any builders or contractors for bidding purposes. They will also serve as guides for the actual construction.

Now is the time to select a contractor. This may be someone the architect has previously worked with or someone recommended through a personal referral. Get three bids on the job, if at all possible. Research the contractor's previous work, and select someone with whom you feel you can work comfortably.

When you choose your contractor, you will work out a contract that spells out starting and estimated completion dates, cost (a lump sum or time-and-materials), payment schedule, site access, hours of construction, policies regarding change orders during construction, cleanup, and other factors.

■ **CONSTRUCTION PHASE.** Your dreams are about to become reality! Once permits have been obtained and you've selected your contractor or builder (if applicable), it's time for actual construction to begin. This can be an involved process unless the project is very simple, but if you keep on top of it at all stages, the results will be well worth it.

If you're doing the work yourself, you'll be responsible for ordering and buying materials, hiring any subcontractors, setting schedules, and arranging for inspections. Otherwise, the general contractor will take care of these aspects, and you (and your architect, if there is one) will work with the contractor on making decisions and handling the problems that inevitably crop up. A final inspection by the building department will be required on completion.

Understanding Architectural Drawings

Architects commonly work with and produce three basic types of drawings. Sometimes additional 3-D drawings may be created.

Plans are the basic tool for planning. A plan may show anything from an entire neighborhood to a single built-in bench; it may be a site plan, a floor plan, an enlarged plan of a single room, and so forth. Essentially, it's a bird's-eye view—a flattened view seen from above. Plans include the horizontal dimensions of the building and its rooms.

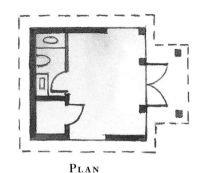

PLAN

Sections show a profile of a building or a detail of a building; they make a visual "cut" vertically through the building or detail. (Similarly, a site section shows a cut through the earth, especially a hill, as shown on page 15.) Sections are a good tool for understanding the interior spaces and construction system of a building. They may include cross sections and lengthwise sections of the entire building as well as wall sections and sections of details such as built-in cabinets. These drawings include vertical dimensions, or heights and changes in level, explaining visually how spaces relate to one another.

ELEVATION

Elevations show you a building or a room as if you are standing directly back and looking at it; they may include views from different directions, conveying the building's general appearance and scale. There are exterior and interior elevations and enlarged detail elevations showing elements such as roofing, moldings, fireplaces, windows, or doors.

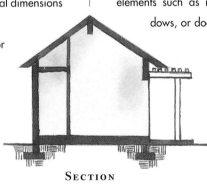

SECTION

3-D views, which are less common, are sometimes used for preliminary design work. They help you visualize what an interior or exterior will look like by representing it in perspective—from above, from a distance, or from an angle. More difficult and time-consuming to produce, they are not usually provided with working drawings.

3-D VIEWS

ISOMETRIC DRAWING

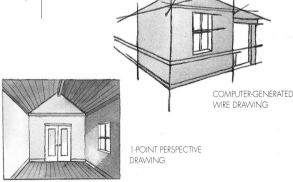

1-POINT PERSPECTIVE DRAWING

COMPUTER-GENERATED WIRE DRAWING

planning your cottage

a matter of style

COTTAGE STYLE, *for one person, might mean the picture of old-fashioned charm associated with cottages of bygone times. For someone else, it might be something quite different. A quick look at some style considerations is presented here to inspire you as you think about your own cottage.*

Style grab bag

Traditionally cottages have been unassuming little dwellings. Many older cottages were built as vacation homes or even as outbuildings on large estates. But historically cottages have also been main residences for people of modest means. In the past they were often constructed of local materials—stone from the rocky countryside, logs from surrounding forests—although they also might be built with wood shingles or other conventional materials. Reflecting their traditional position outside the mainstream of fashion and design, cottages tend to be casually furnished—even a bit quirky—with a friendly mix of hand-me-downs and inexpensive furniture, memorabilia and flea market finds.

These days, the cottage in your backyard can be any style you choose. It will naturally have the small scale and possibly the easy, casual approach common to traditional cottages, but there the resemblance may end. Your cottage may be built in the image of a tiny Greek tem-

The ageless simplicity of Japanese architecture inspired this small teahouse. Hallmarks of its style are the open sides, shoji screens, sloping roofline, and natural-finish wood.

ple, or it may be a rustic-looking log cabin or a gingerbread Victorian mansion in miniature. You may opt for the look of a Japanese teahouse or for a small but sleek contemporary structure.

In fact, because a backyard cottage can be less "serious" than a main dwelling, you may want to have a little fun with its design—to create something you would love but feel you can't do with your main residence. Perhaps you've always harbored a secret desire for a Hansel and Gretel fairytale cottage—or a wildly contemporary, all-glass studio. Unless you think you'll run into problems with your neighbors or your local design review board, you can let yourself go when it comes to style.

To match or not to match?

You may want your cottage to echo the lines, colors, and style of your house, especially if the two are close together. Some styles are more flexible than others. A shingled Cape Cod house might call for a cottage in the same style, whereas a stucco ranch house might blend with a wider range of cottage styles.

Sometimes you can suggest a connection between your main and accessory buildings by using a unifying element, such as similar roof lines, window styles, siding, or trim colors.

You probably don't want to build a rustic potting shed a stone's throw from an elegant Georgian-style home, or a formal-looking cabana across the pool from a cabin-style home. But with enough separation between cottage and main house, you can build something that is a departure in design. Skillful handling and design will make the difference between a successful marriage of styles and an awkward one.

Foundations of style

All the components you choose for constructing your cottage—from the framing and roofing to the flooring and siding—carry out a certain kind of style. Deciding on the basic construction technique will be an important step toward firming up the general style of your cottage. The

The many-windowed summerhouse above has an unmistakable air of elegance, thanks to its shape as well as its decorative trim, hardware, and stained glass. At left, the inimitable style of a free spirit is expressed in a hideaway approached through a colorful archway. The artist owner displays original work and found objects on the cottage door.

basic framing component of a cottage, like that of a house, can be any of these:

- Conventional wood stud framing
- Masonry (brick, stone, concrete block, adobe)
- Alternative construction (rammed earth, straw bale, metal stud)

Wood-frame houses are the most common and most versatile; they may be finished with a cladding, or siding, of various materials. Wood siding—such as shingles or boards—is most widely chosen. But decorative brick or stone, stucco, metal, or even glass can be used on wood frame construction.

A masonry structure of stone, brick, or adobe has its own unique character, while alternative construction techniques such as rammed earth might give a quite different look.

Materials and finishes

You'll face myriad choices among elements such as roof styles and roofing materials, siding, doors, windows, skylights, paint, trim, hardware, and embellishments (cupolas, shutters, and weathervanes, for example). Although making these

The spirit of the Carpenter Gothic wooden house, which evolved in the mid-1800s from Methodist campground cottages, is expressed in this little gem, festooned with gingerbread trim and brightened with a creative paint scheme.

Weathered wood shakes and shingles, recycled wood shutters and door, a simple stone for a doorstep—all contribute to a rustic look, set off by a basket of blooms.

choices can be bewildering, it's also fun, since this is what creates the character of your cottage.

A traditional peaked-roof structure clad in wooden shingles, with shutters at the windows and a vine-covered trellis alongside the front door, is the essence of the old-fashioned cottage. A shed-roofed mini-tower painted in primary colors makes another statement, a classic Monticello-style brick cottage yet another. For a look at many choices, turn to the section beginning on page 99.

Interior style

No matter what activities you plan to pursue in your cottage, you undoubtedly want the indoor space to be beautiful and pleasant as well as practical. In an art or crafts studio, for example, clarity of light may be of paramount importance. Skylights and lots of windows may be called for to let in maximum light.

The charm of a Swedish log dwelling inhabits an artfully framed sleeping enclosure (left). Below, bold use of color imparts a sense of fun, while a work-room's creative clutter (bottom) provides inspiration for its artist owner.

No doubt you also want your cottage to be a place where you can really express yourself. Perhaps you've always wanted a room painted bright yellow, but no one in your family wants that color in the main house. You can have your sunny walls in this special cottage. Or if your main house is a friendly but sometimes over-whelming hodgepodge of family clutter, you might want a retreat that's perfectly serene—no furniture at all, just some Japanese-style matting on a polished wood floor and light streaming in the open door. Or maybe you want to create a little bit of Provence in a summerhouse meant for dining and entertaining, complete with an old wooden hutch to hold dishes and a long, scrubbed wood dining table. For a look at many options, turn to the following two chapters.

A GALLERY OF COTTAGES

GETTING INSPIRED is one of the first—and most enjoyable—steps on the path toward creating a cottage in your backyard. You may already be focused about the style and design you want, or you may still be in the early stages of dreaming and idea gathering. Either way, you'll find plenty to spark your imagination in the array of photos offered in this chapter. **ARRANGED ACCORDING TO THE USES THEY SERVE,** the cottages we show you in these pages range from delightful hideaways for reading and relaxing to pretty playhouses for children and charming guest quarters that will have your friends clamoring for a visit. Just for fun, we also feature some lighthearted approaches—out-of-the-ordinary designs, for example, and little backyard homes for pets. **AS YOU BROWSE,** consider both the use you envision for your own space and the designs that especially appeal to you. Who knows? One of the ideas you find here may set you on your way to making your cottage dream come true.

34

relaxing
retreats

A COTTAGE DESIGNED just for relaxation makes "getting away from it all" as easy as going out into your own backyard. Whether it's a tiny room just big enough for one person or a gracious space large enough for a gathering of friends or family, such a retreat feels like pure indulgence.

You have your choice when it comes to complexity of construction. You may opt for a simple enclosure to be used mostly for lounging and reading during the daytime, with only a comfortable chair and windows open to the breeze and no need for electricity or running water. Or you may want something a little more elaborate—a spacious, comfortable "living room" complete with lights, a fireplace, and perhaps a wet bar.

Here's your chance to exercise your creativity, since the whole point is to design a special space that appeals to your sense of aesthetics as well as comfort. As you'll see on the following pages, your personal retreat can resemble a fishing cabin or an old-fashioned screened porch, a garden pavilion or an elegant great room. The choice is all yours.

An old pump house in a neglected back corner of the owner's property has been transformed into an elegantly simple retreat, now a welcoming destination in the garden— especially in the evening, when its lights beckon. The cottage is set close to boundary fences, but setback requirements were not an issue because this was a remodel of an existing structure.

Craftsman-style French doors open into a serene space handsomely floored in mahogany and furnished in utter simplicity.

A unique ceiling treatment that follows the roof peak was created with bamboo poles, conferring architectural distinction and evoking the feeling of a quieter time and place.

*Perched on a dock at the edge of a duck pond,
this buoyant little boathouse measures just 10 by
10 feet yet packs in miles of style. The interior,
featuring paddles, a carved wood salmon, and a
collection of lures, reflects the owner-builders' love
of fishing; the cheery color palette adds to the sense
of fun and relaxation.*

*A bell-shaped roof, custom-made from copper, lends distinctive European style
to the handsome octagonal garden house below. Cooling breezes and garden
fragrances waft in through the many doors and windows.*

A charming reading
retreat (facing page)
began with an old well,
over which the owner
built a wood floor and
an arbor (its beams
and rafters are still
visible inside). Walls, a
gabled roof, and a
brick floor came later.
Materials are a
delightful hodgepodge
of recycled lumber,
shingles, and windows,
including vintage glass
block. For an interior
view, see page 98.

Its creator dubbed this breezy retreat a
"folly"—a whimsical little structure.
The freestanding screened "porch" rises from
a native-stone foundation in a tree-shaded
field. Wicker furnishings, bamboo shades,
and antiqued board cupboards reinforce
the friendly style.

Constructed of weather-resistant natural cedar inside and out, this modest little house blends effortlessly with its surroundings. Designed for relaxing before or after a swim in the nearby pool (not visible), it offers comfy wicker furnishings that invite chatting, plus a tiny adjacent kitchen and changing room.

An old tractor shed, built circa 1790, is now an airy gathering place. Its sculptor-owner concocted the "relief" on the original roll-back barn doors from lumber scraps; the big table was made from old attic floorboards. A clear polycarbonate plastic overhang shields the doorway from rain. In winter, the owner simply packs up the furniture and lets the snow blow through.

in the treetops

FOR THE CHILD IN US, there's probably nothing more appealing than the idea of a secret hideout nestled among the branches of a beloved tree. From the Swiss Family Robinson to contemporary creators of treetop home offices, adventurous spirits just naturally take to the trees.

A treehouse can be literally up a tree, supported by a system of beams and cables, or it can be closer to the ground yet framed and even partially supported by tree trunks or limbs. It may be a simple roofed platform with safety railings all around or a multiroom dwelling complete with heat, light, and all the comforts of home—or something in between. Access can be rough-and-ready (a simple ladder) or more "civilized" (a flight of stairs complete with landings at various levels).

Before embarking on construction, you'll need to do some basic fact-finding. Although a simple, close-to-the-ground treehouse may not be subject to the same regulations as a conventional structure, it's a good idea to check with your local building department for guidance. You should also be aware of such crucial considerations as the choice and treatment of the "host" tree, the safety and stability of the structure itself, and safe access from the ground. And if children will be using the treehouse, adequate supervision must be provided. You can find help in the many books and articles available about treehouses.

Massive redwood trunks are essential to the character, if not the actual structure, of the rustic sleeping pavilion at right. It began as a gazebo, accessible over decking in a wooded lakefront garden; now it houses a bed designed to be taken apart and stored in winter. At left, a simple house was built above the stump when the main part of an old bay tree died. Nestled among the suckers that grew up around it, the house is reached by steps in back.

This handsome treehouse, dubbed "Reynolds' Folly," wraps right around a backyard tree. The owner's son climbs a rope ladder to the porch; a wire trolley lets him zip over to another tree.

gardeners' hideaways

AN AIR OF FRIENDLY CHARM imbues many gardeners' hideaways, whether they function as working garden sheds or as informal garden rooms meant for relaxation, too. Those that house all the gritty elements of gardening—pots, bags of soil, garden tools and equipment, flats of seedlings—must be practical, down-to-earth structures that can take some hard knocks. Yet many garden cottages are also havens for garden putterers—places where their owners love to spend their leisure time. As such, they often express the unique personality and style of their inhabitants.

A working potting shed requires an ample counter or workbench for potting; storage shelves or cupboards for pots, tools, and other equipment; and perhaps containers for soil, fertilizer, and so on. If you'll start seedlings or winter plants in your shed, you'll need windows that let in adequate light. An important requirement is running water, either from a nearby hose bibb or from a sink plumbed into the shed. The floor must be practical, too; a simple on-grade floor of loose-laid bricks or pavers or of pea gravel will generally give secure footing yet allow for water runoff.

A garden cottage meant for relaxation (at least some of the time) can take a variety of aesthetic directions. Lots of windows can make the space light and pleasant, as long as there's also provision for shade on hot days. Decorative touches might include bright paint, decorative garden accessories, and even the pots themselves.

Seen through the frame of a rose arbor behind the main house, this potting shed appears as a delightful surprise in the landscape. It's usefully situated directly across from the vegetable garden.

Built from recycled wood and wire screening, a roomy potting bench offers plenty of counter space as well as open shelves above and below for storage. A brightly stenciled paint job gives it personality. Note the creative storage and decorative details, including hanging tiered baskets, a grocer's scale, and whimsical garden ornaments.

The bright yellow doors, with their surrounding molding of electric blue, extend a cheery welcome into the shed's light-filled interior. Except for the weatherproof metal doors and the acrylic roofing, only recycled construction materials were used. The "floor" is a crunchy layer of practical pea gravel.

Here's a working garden shed that's also a wonderful private place to take a break. The big window (salvaged from a construction project) looks out onto a "secret garden" and stone obelisk. The sliding barn door (below) allows easy access for garden equipment—and for the children who love to play inside.

This appealing shed is the busy center from which the owner maintains a six-acre garden. Built-in counters and shelves and a big wooden table provide plenty of work surfaces. A century-old chicken-ranch workers' house, the cottage has been given a face-lift inside and out yet retains its rustic character. Besides providing storage space for garden equipment, it's a mini-gallery for seed packet art.

Perspective belies the true scale of this little white garden

house and storage shed. It started life as a duck house; the

Dutch door (originally a window) is barely people-size.

Remodeling the shed was a family project for the owners, as

is the garden of ornamental vegetables and cutting flowers.

Created from recycled materials—old wooden storm windows, used fence posts, salvaged nursery potting tables, even white birch for beams—this light, bright retreat-cum-potting shed is a haven for its owner, an avid gardener. In winter, she heats the space with a portable plug-in radiator and snuggles up with seed catalogs. In summer, the trees shade the space and open doors admit cooling breezes.

home at work

THE HOME OFFICE, it seems, is here to stay. For many of us, working at home is our best option; we can be near our families, avoid long commutes, and work in a peaceful, semi-secluded environment. Even those whose jobs take them away during the day may find a home office a necessity for work overflow in the evenings and on weekends.

A backyard cottage can be the perfect solution. Be it a converted garage or a brand-new structure, a detached home office gives just the right degree of separation between your home life and your work life. Whether you're a writer, a marketing consultant, or an entrepreneur running a small business, you can set up an office that meets your particular needs while also functioning as an attractive part of your landscape. On these pages you'll see examples of both simple and elaborate structural design, with varying interior styles.

Aesthetics aside, essential elements are electricity, heat (in most climates), phone and Internet connections, and adequate work surfaces and storage. (It's nice to have a bathroom and a place to make a cup of coffee or tea, but these may not be necessities.) Measure the things you'll need and use on a regular basis, from computer and fax machine to chair and file cabinets, and plan on plenty of space for office supplies.

A two-story plan multiplies the usable area of this backyard structure. The owner-architect's studio is upstairs (facing page); below are a small bath, kitchenette, and bedroom.

Tucked under the gable roof, this architect's work space receives lots of natural light through a skylight and windows at both ends, augmented by good-looking light fixtures. A built-in desk and a broad ledge running around the room offer maximum work surface in a tiny space. Light washes of color on pine and spruce board paneling echo the color of sky and trees, giving this serene space the feeling of a nest among the trees.

Outdoors it's cold and snowy, but inside this backyard cottage office the atmosphere is cozy. Although furnishings are spare, as befits the serious working space of this writer and editor, the natural wood paneling, rug, and shelves of books create a warm feeling. The design makes efficient use of the tiny area by utilizing built-ins— a wrap-around work surface, bookshelves, and compartments sized for computer components.

The simple wood-shingled cottage fits naturally into its woodsy setting. Large awning windows on facing walls let in winter light when surrounding tree branches are bare; in summer leafy boughs will shade the little cottage and help keep it cool, especially when the windows are propped open to admit breezes.

Coming upon this writer's haven is meant to feel like discovering a hidden workshop deep in the woods. You enter by stages: past the trellised pavilion into an open space, then into the studio itself. With their barrel roofs, office and pavilion give a mirror-image impression; the trellised pavilion wall echoes the office's divided-light doors and windows. Sophisticated simplicity characterizes the interior space. French doors and generous window area allow forest light to play in pleasing patterns over natural fir flooring.

Inside the compact office space, work surfaces and storage cabinets are neatly organized for maximum efficiency. An original take on recycling is the countertop, made from a salvaged wood bowling alley surface.

Rather than lose planting space on her small urban lot, the owner of this architect's studio moved her garden upward. Flowers and grasses grow on the roof in 5 inches of soil over a waterproof membrane. Drip irrigation waters the drought-tolerant plants. Floor-to-ceiling windows and a Dutch door are among recycled construction materials; shingles are sustainably harvested redwood.

just for fun

LUCKY THE CHILD who has a playhouse of his or her own. Though even an empty refrigerator box can be a fun hideaway, a playhouse built to order is a dream come true.

Options range from designing and building a playhouse yourself to ordering one premade (finished or in kit form) or having it custom-designed. Adding details is part of the fun. Playhouses are perfect candidates for fanciful little porches, decorative trim, Dutch doors, and window boxes.

Follow the same safety guidelines you would follow for any room in which children will be playing. Provide plenty of ventilation, and make sure doors and windows can't lock shut, trapping children inside. If there are windows, use tempered glass or plastic. And there's no substitute for adult supervision—you will probably want to site your playhouse where you can easily watch it from the house.

Built to an adequate scale, your playhouse can become a home office or a guest cottage when the kids are grown. It's important to think through possible future uses during the planning stage so that you can either install necessary utilities when you build the playhouse or make it easy to hook them up later. Keep in mind, too, that an office or guest cottage may require a more permanent foundation than a playhouse meant to last only a few years.

Sporting all the architectural details of a full-size country cottage, this playhouse was purchased ready-made. Inside, a child-size ladder leads to a loft with its own window on the world.

The dream of a playhouse at right is enhanced by a wealth of decorative play-yard accents, from birdhouse to railroad-car planter. Note how the exterior details— dormer windows, porch railing, lanterns, windows, and trim— are perfectly scaled to playhouse size.

Upstairs is for kids, downstairs for dogs!
Go through a crayon-bright Dutch door and you're
greeted by a cozy play space complete with a table
set for tea. The playhouse "basement" is ready for
a real canine occupant or a plush pet.

a style tour

REGIONAL STYLES OF ARCHITECTURE are powerful icons that allow us to instantly conjure up an image of a particular place. Think of Tuscany, and you see clay-tiled roofs above the faded gold of peeling, sun-washed stucco walls; rural Midwest America brings to mind images of red barns in an agricultural sea of green. Building a backyard cottage gives you the opportunity to re-create a particular regional style that appeals to you, whether it evokes childhood memories, recalls a memorable travel destination, or reflects the distinctive style of the area in which you live.

Often people feel freer to play with regional style when building a small backyard structure than they would in building a main residence. You'll find cottages with echoes of regional styles throughout this book—see, for example, the Asian-inspired shelter on page 28. And on these four pages we've assembled a small sampling of cottages that come right out and make bold reference to distinctive geographic influences in the United States and Europe.

Since the earliest European settlements in North America, the log cabin has been a symbol of this country's frontier spirit. This version shares the compact size and essential simplicity of its forerunners; its decor is a lighthearted take on classic country and folk elements that includes rustic hand-crafted furniture, a Native American rug, "homespun" textiles— even a "trophy" chandelier.

Designed as a playhouse, this little log cabin is pure fun for kids and grown-ups alike.

A tiny adobe shelter set into a Santa Fe garden wall pays homage to architectural traditions of the American Southwest. Vegetation sprouts at its feet and on its roof, emphasizing the connection between the clay-and-sand building material and the earth from which it "grows."

It could be in England's Cotswolds, but this evocative guest cottage is actually in California. Like its English models, it's constructed of local stone; the shingled roof, with its rounded contours and deep eaves, has the look of thatching. Arched leaded glass windows set into thick stone walls are also typical of the traditional English stone cottage.

Enter the cobbled courtyard of this
vine-covered garden cottage and you
might think you were in Tuscany (though
it's really the northeastern United States).
Inside and out, the owner-designer's
passion for antique architectural fragments
and garden ornaments creates a flavor of
bygone romance combined with
contemporary flair.

creature comforts

FOR DEDICATED DOG LOVERS, that special backyard cottage just might be a doghouse. After all, don't our canine companions deserve the best? Its size makes this a good do-it-yourself project—if every scrap of lumber isn't sawed perfectly, will your dog complain? And since the inherent nature of doghouses is a bit on the whimsical side in the first place, this is the perfect opportunity to have fun with design. Want a Wild West town in miniature? A pooch-size lighthouse? Or how about a miniature Southwestern-style adobe?

If you don't want to build an elaborate structure, you might enlist your creativity to make use of alternative materials or structures. Outgrown children's playhouses have been converted into generous-size kennels. One inventive soul turned a clean wooden wine barrel on its side, added supports at the bottom, and thereby created the serviceable and good-looking doghouse shown on the facing page. Here we show you a few ideas to inspire you to design your own doggy digs.

On the fancy side of doghouse design, inventive approaches abound. At left, a small-scale lighthouse replica is one pooch's haven; below, Franny and Zoey share an elegant patio "lean-to" complete with topiary accents.

An entire Wild West
street scene offers doggone
fine accommodations for
two canine pardners.

A humble wine barrel,
"remodeled" as a canine cottage,
is a comfy spot for a snooze.

People love this
fanciful dwelling—
dubbed the "Bowhaus"
by its designer—as
much as its occupant
does! With its perky
contours, decorative
trim, and bold color
created with weather-
resistant tung-oil stains,
it really brightens up
the landscape.

art in process

A PAINTER, A SCULPTOR, a potter, a fabric artist—
anyone who works with the visual arts—longs at some point for
a special place for germinating the seeds of creative ideas and
bringing them to fruition. It's probably not just the space and solitude
you crave, either—it's the chance to make free with all of your "stuff." Bags of
clay and jars of brushes, piles of fabric, canvases on stretchers, kilns, easels,
soldering irons—all the delightful clutter necessary for making art—take up
room. You need the freedom to leave these things out instead of stashing them
away every time a room is needed for more mundane pursuits.

In its wooded Maine setting, this rustic potter's studio looks like a natural part of the landscape. Peeled tree trunks support the roof of the porch, where shelves display the artist's wares.

Whether your studio is a reclaimed garage or a custom-built artist's cottage,
practical requirements depend on how you will use the space. A watercolorist
might need little more than room for an easel, paints, and paper, whereas a potter requires a kiln, a potter's wheel, and generous work and storage surfaces.
Take stock of your needs: the size and type of work surface (a long table for cutting fabrics, a counter for framing pictures), storage, and display space (if you'll
use your studio as a mini-gallery, too).

The refined potting studio at right— a renovated barn— welcomes visitors with a handsome façade draped in potato vine. Its symmetry, along with the spare gravel courtyard, gives a slightly formal feeling. The studio's 100-year-old redwood siding came from another building on the property; the old barn door has been installed above the new French doors.

Interior surfaces—especially flooring—most likely will
need to be able to withstand
hard use, spills, and splatters.
As for utilities, you may or
may not need running water,
but you will almost certainly
want a generous helping of
light, natural and artificial. Be
judicious in placing windows
and skylights so that you will
have light where you want it,
not glaring onto your work.

Inside the serene work
space, bathed in cool
light, a potter's kiln
gleams in one corner;
shelves hold completed
pieces. Work surfaces
and storage are
combined tidily in units
like the one pictured
at left.

Tall French doors swing wide to reveal an airy, light-filled studio within this rustic wood building. The spare interior houses a potter's kiln and equipment; the white walls also make a good place to tack up photos for critiquing.

Cement floors can take the hard knocks that are sometimes a product of the artistic process. Skylights bathe the space in light; cables support utilitarian artificial lighting. A stainless steel sink is a practical addition.

Step through an arched courtyard door and you've entered the artist-owner's special universe. Enveloped in blooming plants, the stucco cottage has the clay-tile roof typical of Mediterranean buildings. Inside, the studio features a fireplace and a bed, so it can double as a guest cottage.

*At the end of a winding
path from the main
house, a studio is both
painter's work space
and gallery. Inside
(left), the northern
exposure affords clear,
nonglaring light from
skylights, windows,
and glass doors; track
lights spotlight works
on display. A loft (out
of view) affords
storage; an adjoining
finished garage adds
more display space.*

*In the South, a screened porch is de rigueur, letting summer
breezes in and keeping pesky mosquitoes out—so a screened
cottage makes perfect sense. Here at a bend in a path between
the main house and a creek, the artist-owner is often at work
with a small easel and paints. Railings around the screen
walls are perfect for displaying her miniature canvases.*

taking the plunge

IF YOU HAVE A SWIMMING POOL on your property, your enjoyment—and that of your guests—will be greatly enhanced by having a pool house close at hand. Such a building adds a whole extra level of comfort and convenience, usually in the form of a bathroom and shower and a changing room—lots better than running in and out the back door, trailing water and wet towels through the house. A pool house can be a wonderful asset for entertaining, too, whether you simply install a fridge for cold drinks and snacks or (space and budget permitting) add a small kitchen, a barbecue, and perhaps an indoor or outdoor dining area.

Practicalities aside, a pool house can also be lovely to look at. A handsome cottage at one end of a pool provides a focal point in the landscape; an appealing reflection in the pool waters often is a bonus. Hiding equipment away within the pool house contributes to making the area attractive, too. Good-looking paving, fencing, and plantings extending to and around the pool house can effectively link main house, pool house, pool, and landscape elements into one unified picture.

At the edge of a free-form pool, this gem of a pool house immediately draws the eye with its bright white trim and unusual roof line. The rippled mirror image of the structure doubles its appeal.

Like the prow of a liner about to set sail, the tiny porch of this two-story pool house juts forward toward the water. Climbing the stairway suggests embarking up a ship's gangplank. Shingled in classic Cape Cod style, the structure is screened upstairs to make a cool and comfortable summer guest room. Tucked below are a bathroom and handy storage space for pool paraphernalia.

Surrounded by a sea of gardens and shrubbery, the pool area is bounded by a rustic wood fence that perfectly complements the style of the house. Perennial borders bloom at its feet; copper post caps repeat the shape of the cottage's hip roof, seen above.

In the changing room, clean white walls and a slatted wood bench provide practical surfaces for dripping swimmers and their gear. The space is pleasantly sunny and bright; hopper windows ventilate the room without directing chilling breezes downward.

A safety feature can also contribute style to the landscape, as evidenced by the picket fence. The arbor above the entry gate adds a welcoming grace note and encourages flowering vines to climb up its latticed sides.

The style of the main house—an 18th-century saltbox—is echoed in the dormer windows, white-painted shingles and siding, and handsome pergola of the pool house. A central portal leads toward tennis courts. On one side are bathroom, changing room, and kitchenette; the other side holds pool equipment, games, and, in winter, the patio furniture.

ready-made style

a gallery of cottages

THANKS TO THE MANY mail-order plans and even prefabricated buildings available today, a backyard cottage may be easier to own than you think. You have a broad array of choices, from elegant prefabricated glass conservatories to simple sheds sold as kits or guest cottage plans that you send away for.

If you choose one of the more elaborate prefabricated shelters, you may begin by consulting with a design professional associated with the manufacturer. This person may help with everything from obtaining building permits to adapting the design to your specifics, then building and installing the structure on site.

At the other end of the spectrum, you may order plans for a shed or cottage from a home improvement book or magazine, then build it yourself or with professional help. Or you may purchase a kit—complete with precut wood, hardware, and instructions—from a building or home improvement center or through the Internet, a catalog, or a book. Some structures, such as children's playhouses, can be ordered ready-made. They'll be shipped in prefabricated parts to be unloaded and set up on a foundation by the company or by you.

Whatever route you take, you must still do your homework regarding siting considerations and code requirements, as described on pages 20–21. And don't forget that every cottage needs a foundation; together with any utilities you want, this adds to the expense and complexity of the project.

This prefab garden shed was trucked to its site already assembled. Note the double doors and ramp for wheeling large and heavy items in and out. The owners' own charming touches include a birdhouse tucked below the roof.

The interior of the kit-built tent bungalow at right has a unique ornithological theme, thanks to a talented decorative artist. Furnishings bring to mind 19th-century naturalists' field expeditions, during which the comforts of home—even Oriental rugs—lent a feeling of permanence to temporary dwellings.

Combining the fun of camping
with the comfort of a cottage, a
good-looking prefab tent
bungalow sits securely atop a
wooden platform. Waterproof
laminated vinyl walls are
supported on a wood or metal
frame. "Civilized" components
include wood-frame windows
and door.

*Built from mail-order plans, this jewel of a cottage is an
irresistible spot for relaxing. Only 9 by 12 feet, it's made of
stock materials purchased at a home center. Key to the design
are standard oak French doors, installed upside down
and hinged on top to be used as windows; dowels prop them
open to let in breezes. One-of-a-kind furnishings and
collectibles give the interior its unique character.*

An elegant prefabricated glass house recalls its Victorian ancestors in details like ornamental ridge cresting on the roof. Surrounded by white roses and lemon trees, it's a striking garden destination.

The owners customized the interior space for use as a potting shed, adding a wooden work counter complete with sink and an old stone trough to hold potting soil. On a sunny day, it's a particular pleasure to work in this light-filled room.

pure whimsy

SOMETIMES IT'S GOOD FOR THE SOUL to abandon practicality and have a little old-fashioned fun. What better way to express the spirit of fun than to create a backyard fantasy all your own? That's what the cottages pictured here are all about.

Whether you like your dose of whimsy on the subtle side or over the top, you can find creative ways to express it with siding, paint, and doodads, as these homeowners have done. Perhaps your cottage style will be an expression of a passionate interest (such as trains or boats), or maybe it will represent in miniature a beloved locale (real or imaginary, from a favorite book or movie). As long as you don't transgress neighborhood rules (written and unwritten), you can feel free to go ahead and have a good time!

This slightly off-kilter version of a storybook cottage is just plain fun. (Its playful exterior belies its practical function as a garden shed.) While some elements—like the crooked chimney pipe and skewed windows— are clearly goofy, the basic structure is just regular enough to keep it from looking like a mistake. The surrounding flowers are just the right scale.

A train station in the garden? Or how about a tugboat? A love of rail-road lore inspired the decor for the cottage at right, reminiscent of an old-time rural train depot. Below right, an actual cabin from an old tug has been outfitted as a potting shed. And a real chicken coop, decked out with vintage signs and mini-windmill, adds a playful touch to the landscape below left.

a gallery of cottages

come to stay

FROM A COZY CABIN in the woods to an elegant poolside getaway, guest cottages of every stripe say "Welcome!" These little homes-away-from-home can range from the most basic of shelters to fully equipped small houses. You can erect a simple sleeping cottage just big enough for a bed and a chair, or you can pull out all the stops and offer your guests a dwelling complete with living room, bedroom, bath, and even a small kitchen.

Obviously, a "full-service" guest cottage is a large project—akin to building a house, on a smaller scale. In addition to requiring a generous amount of property, it calls for a complete complement of utilities and indoor accoutrements—fixtures, appliances, furnishings. But the beauty of such a cottage is its versatility. Sometime in the future, it might become a dwelling for an older child or an aging relative, or it could bring in income as a rental unit if local zoning ordinances allow that. When you apply for permits and building department approval (see pages 20–21), you'll want to plan ahead regarding any such possibilities.

Whether your accommodations are to be simple or elaborate, think of the fun you'll have decorating for your guests! Make clever use of an overflow of furniture and decor from your main house, or put together a collection of new or flea-market finds. Go elegant or go zany; pick up on a theme, be it tropical island or Old Mexico; or go for an intriguing color palette. And have fun with accessories—playful signs, perhaps, or your collection of souvenir plates or teddy bears. The things that charm you are bound to charm your guests, too.

A modest entrance conveys a cozy feeling the minute you step inside. Tongue-and-groove paneling, Shaker-style pegs for hanging jackets, and firewood stacked under a simple bench all be-speak casual warmth.

Designed as an artist's studio and guest quarters, this cottage inhabits its setting with natural grace. Clap-board siding and roof shingles of untreated Western red cedar will weather to a soft silver. The tall chimney and the small, square windows under the eaves give the structure timeless cottage appeal. On the opposite side, large windows face out on a harbor.

The main living area centers on a fireplace of local granite. Among the simple, comfortable furnishings are a daybed handcrafted by the owner's son and a built-in desk and storage unit. Bedroom, bath, and kitchenette are around the corner.

It's a slice of the tropics—on an urban lot in Northern California!
Everything about this retreat is designed to make guests smile, from
the diminutive front porch to the banana-yellow paint to the funky
galvanized roof, reminiscent of a Pacific island beach hut. The
cabana was created using redwood from a derelict shed; the banana
tree, growing in a tangle of shrubbery, inspired the style.

Out the side door, a tiny patio offers a shaded spot to relax with a cup of tea—or perhaps a rum punch. In keeping with the beach feeling, the structure's design encourages ready movement between indoors and outdoors.

Iridescent netting—a colorful take on tropical mosquito netting—surrounds the handmade camp-style bed. The bare floor is cool underfoot and easy to clean.

*Offering all the comforts of home, this Craftsman-style bungalow
has a bedroom tucked under the dormer and a living area with
pocket doors that can open the entire wall to the outdoors.*

*The bungalow's focal point is the generously
proportioned Colorado bluestone fireplace,
with its built-in display niche. Guests can cozy
up to the hearth in the cool of the evening, then
fling open the doors when a warm day dawns.*

Warm and welcoming, the interior packs a lot into a small space. A tiny dining area adjoins the living room (above), connecting with the compact kitchen through French windows that can be left open or closed to set off the space. Paneling and woodwork in rich natural redwood pull it all together. At one end of the living area, a bank of casement windows (left) opens onto the garden. A bathroom is tucked to one side.

With wood smoke curling from its chimney pipe, a tiny cabin in the woods beckons invitingly across the snowy expanse. The pavilion roof, practical for shedding snow, accommodates a skylit sleeping loft (below). Doors slide open to a deck. A wood stove keeps the entire space toasty even when the mercury drops at night.

The cozy bedroom, like the rest of the interior, is paneled in classic knotty pine; traditional bedding and a braided rug add warm color. The furnishings are spare, as befits a casual ski cabin, and the simplicity of the interior allows the eye to focus on the winterscape outside the windows.

Interiors depicted in the works of Swedish painter Carl Larsson inspired the decor. The painted floral motifs, as well as the cream-and-soft-green color scheme, are hallmarks of Larsson's visual world. Curling up on the window seat at right, with its built-in bookshelves, is an experience every guest anticipates.

This tree-shaded cottage invites lucky guests to wander at will, in through the wide sliding pocket doors or out onto the brick patio. A low roof line, overhanging eaves, and small-paned windows create classic cottage appeal.

Elements from beloved bygone eras enliven the interior. In the tiny kitchen (left), a restored Wedgwood stove and 1930s-style cabinetry set the tone. In the living-dining area (above), the vintage jukebox and neon clock from the 1950s bestow a lighthearted atmosphere. Tongue-and-groove paneling is used throughout.

made for entertaining

CANDLELIGHT DINNERS under the stars, pool house barbecues, cozy fireside gatherings—any kind of get-together feels special in a backyard-cottage setting. Backyard entertaining places may be fully enclosed dwellings that double as pool houses, retreats, or guest cottages, or they may be more informal, partially roofed and walled structures—or even enclosures within patio walls that become defined as entertainment areas.

Some entertainment spaces have cooking facilities—full kitchens or outdoor barbecue areas. Others may simply be pleasant places to sit for drinks and snacks, or for a luncheon or supper prepared in the main house. Still others may gather folks around a fireplace for intimate talk and relaxation.

Because they are often situated in a lovely garden or poolside setting, backyard entertaining venues offer an atmosphere where everybody feels relaxed. And if an occasion calls for a large guest list, a backyard cottage often allows for free movement between indoors and out.

Whatever form your entertaining structure takes, be sure to provide protection from daytime heat and evening chill as well as a source of light for evening entertaining— candlelight, electric light, or both. You'll want plenty of comfortable seating, along with tables for plates and glasses. And don't be surprised if your guests decide to linger.

Inside, warm tones create a mellowed look. The floor is stained concrete (see page 113 for a closeup). Mixing several stains produced the woodwork color.

Situated next to a vineyard, this handsome structure is at one with its sunwashed surroundings. Spanish influences are clear in the clay-tile roofing, adobe-like golden stucco, peeledwood posts ("vigas") and ceiling beams, and adobe-style fireplaces indoors and out.

*For a unique textured effect,
interior walls were plastered
with taping compound mixed
with straw, then faux-painted.*

The roof of this little dining pavilion seems to float lightly above the "room" below it. Trusses of red cedar support the curved copper; the open space beneath receives natural light from overhead through a strip of translucent plastic at the roof's center. The 8- by 12-foot space is just large enough for a small table and chairs.

Here's the perfect setting for outdoor entertaining—a stone-pillared pavilion with handsome built-in barbecue and hearth. Close at hand inside the multipurpose structure are a kitchenette, a bathroom, and—for sheer luxury—a sauna. In inclement weather, custom-crafted wooden "storm" doors close over the glazed French doors.

Tucked into an intimate courtyard and roofed with an open arbor, this outdoor dining "room" is a gracious setting in which to share a meal with friends. In the evening, candles flicker in the chandelier above the table, while strings of outdoor lights lend sparkle. Close proximity to the house makes serving a breeze.

As stunningly decorated and furnished as any living room
in a principal dwelling, an area designed for entertaining
features a soaring vaulted ceiling, rugged slate tile
flooring, and an entire wall of windows and French doors.
Guests can pull chairs up to the island counter to chat
while drinks and snacks are being prepared in the kitchen.

In the evening with lights aglow, this entertainment cottage is a vision of gracious elegance. The sweeping landscape of mature trees is in keeping with the grandeur of the Palladian façade and the graceful roof line.

Furnishings strike a balance between formality and casual comfort. This table, with its rustic bench, matched lamps, and simple tableau of books and pictures, is a perfect example. It's a natural spot for guests to sit and chat while enjoying the view.

sleeping under the stars

SOME OF US NEVER OUTGROW our delight in sleeping out under the stars. As adults, though, we usually want a little more comfort than the lumpy sleeping bags we dragged out into the back-yard as kids. Build a simple sleeping shelter, and you can have your cake and eat it, too.

As the examples on these pages show, you can be protected from dewdrops and insects yet still be able to fall asleep with the breezes wafting over your face and the stars visible overhead in the night sky. Not only that, but if you opt for a creative design you will have a structure that adds interest to your landscape as well as providing an extra place to accommodate overnight guests.

It's a unique experience to sleep out in this highly original pavilion fashioned of clear acrylic and screening atop a simple 8- by 10-foot wood platform. The transparent walls let dreamers take in the white pines, the stars, and often even deer passing quietly on their way to drink from a nearby pond.

This shelter takes the old-fashioned
sleeping porch and moves it into the
woods, where the sound of breezes in
the trees lulls guests to sleep. The
Victorian-style door and wood-
framed screen "walls" reinforce the
feeling of having turned back the
clock to a simpler time. Visitors pass
through a vine-hung portal formed
by a set of iron doors reclaimed
from a local mine.

COTTAGE ELEMENTS

FROM ITS SHELTERING ROOF to the flowers blooming at its feet, from the curtains at its windows to the furnishings that make it feel like home, each facet of your backyard cottage contributes to its overall look as well as to your own comfort and enjoyment. While this chapter can't examine every detail involved in putting a cottage together, it does aim to provide an overview of options. **FOR YOUR COTTAGE EXTERIOR,** we review what's available today in roofing and siding styles and materials, windows and doors—even trim and embellishments. In addition, we give you a short course on landscaping to help you make your cottage a beautiful and integral feature of your property. **MOVING INDOORS,** we acquaint you with creative wall, floor, and window treatments and provide tips on how to make the most of your space. From this starting point, you can go on to find and install the particular elements that will make your backyard cottage a one-of-a-kind treasure.

Exterior Style

ROOFING, SIDING, WINDOWS, DOORS—AND ALL THE TRIMMINGS

The exterior envelope or "skin" of your cottage serves both essential practical purposes and aesthetic ones. It consists of the basic components of any building—roof, siding, windows and doors, and hardware such as door handles—as well as an almost infinite variety of embellishments. The choices you make among all these elements will help set the style of your cottage as well as make it a solid, weathertight building.

Roofs

The essential part of even the most primitive structure, a roof over our heads is so basic that many of us don't really stop to consider how many forms it can take or what a variety of materials can be used for roofing.

Almost all roofs require a sheathing, or roof deck (usually of plywood or boards), over which the finish material is applied. But beyond this, choices abound. Depending on its design, a roof can give your structure the look of a medieval English cottage, a Southwest desert adobe, or a space-age greenhouse. And as the chart on the facing page illustrates, materials can range from nothing-fancy asphalt shingles to storybook thatching.

This handsome woodshed combines distinctive style with rustic materials; its pavilion roof and siding, both of untrimmed rough-sawn pine, recall hand-hewn early American structures.

ROOF ROUNDUP

Roofs come in many shapes—some traditional, others "invented" by contemporary architects. These are some of the styles commonly used for backyard cottages.

Barrel. Semicylindrical, or curved (see the photo on page 22).
Bell. A roof that has a bell-shaped cross-section (see page 37).
Flat. A roof that has no slope, only a slight pitch to allow for water drainage.
Gable. The classic peaked roof, with two sides sloping downward from a central ridge to form a gable at each end.
Gambrel. Also called *Dutch gable*, a roof with two pitches on each side—as seen on the classic American barn and at right.
Hip. Four sloping sides connected by "hip" joints and meeting in a ridge on top or

forming a pyramid-shaped *pavilion* roof (see photo below).
Shed. A roof with only one pitched plane (see example on page 49).

OVERHEAD OPTIONS

ASPHALT SHINGLES

Asphalt shingle

Made from asphalt-saturated fiberglass or paper mat.
Advantages. One of the least expensive options, readily available in many colors and types.
Disadvantages. Deteriorates more quickly than some materials. As a petroleum by-product, it's not the most environmentally friendly choice.

WOOD SHAKES

Wood shingle/shake

A classic choice either as smooth, uniformly shaped shingles or as more unevenly textured shakes.
Advantages. Contributes natural-style good looks, insulates well.
Disadvantages. Requires diligent maintenance, vulnerable to fire and insects.

Clay or concrete tile

Elongated, curved tiles traditionally shaped from clay, now mostly concrete made to mimic the originals. The classic choice for Southwestern style.
Advantages. Noncombustible, distinctive in style.

Disadvantages. Heavy, expensive, and unsuitable for climates with freeze/thaw cycles.

Metal

Either sheets or shingles that mimic such materials as slate and wood.
Advantages. Noncombustible, durable, and, if made from recycled materials, environmentally friendly.
Disadvantages. Can be complicated and expensive to install.

COPPER

Slate

Time-honored and beautiful, but not always widely available.
Advantages. Durable and noncombustible, with a classic beauty.
Disadvantages. Expensive, heavy; requires maintenance to remain weathertight.

Glass or plastic

Safety glass, acrylic, or the newer clear polycarbonate plastic. Familiar in conservatories and greenhouses, also used in creative contemporary structures (see page 96).

GLASS

Advantages. Gives a bright, open look. Insulates well if double glazed, can facilitate passive solar heating.
Disadvantages. Special framing required to support large expanses of glass safely.

SOD

Sod

Unusual today but once common on the American prairie and in rural Scandinavia, with grass-planted turf atop a normal roof (see page 54).
Advantages. Fun, unique; can have good insulating qualities.
Disadvantages. Tricky to construct, requires vigilant maintenance.

THATCHING

Thatched

An old technique featuring straw, reed, or similar materials fastened together.
Advantages. Has a quaint, traditional cottage look; can be waterproof, provide good insulation.
Disadvantages. Not an option for most people—few artisans know the technique. Vulnerable to fire and insects.

Siding

The outer layer of your walls is every bit as important as the roof in protecting your backyard structure from the weather. But siding offers much more than protection. The materials you choose do much to create the "look" of your structure.

WOOD. By far the most common choice is solid board siding. Among possible variations are *board and batten* (wide boards nailed vertically, their joints covered by narrow strips of wood); *clapboard* (overlapping beveled horizontal boards); and *wood shingles or shakes*. All can be left natural (with sealants applied), stained, or painted.

Wood siding has the great advantage of design flexibility; it can lend your backyard structure the look of a rustic barn, a Japanese teahouse, or a sleek contemporary dwelling. Wood siding is almost always applied to a wood-frame structure, which is first covered with a sheathing of exterior plywood, fiber-board, or gypsum board and often with an additional layer of building paper or the newer "house wrap" material for extra weather protection.

Three types of wood siding—board and batten (top), shingles (center), and clapboard (bottom)—can give cottages very different looks.

PAINT AND STAIN PORTFOLIO

Exterior paint. Oil-based or water-based (latex), exterior paint can be flat, low-luster, semi-gloss, or high-gloss. Usually siding is painted with a flat finish and trim is painted in low-luster or semigloss for durability. In most cases, latex is the paint of choice—it's fast-drying and easy to clean up with soap and water.

Paints can be custom-mixed to any color, or you can choose from a wide array of standard colors. Paint companies often offer preselected palettes to help coordinate trim and siding. Wood must always be painted with a coat of primer before the finish coat is applied.

If insects and spiders are a problem in your yard, ask at your paint store or home improvement center about repellent additives that can be mixed into the paint.

Exterior stain. Stains may be semitransparent or solid-color (opaque). The former contain enough pigment to tint the wood surface but not enough to mask the natural grain completely; they produce a natural, informal look. Solid-color stains are essentially paints; their heavy pigments cover the wood grain completely.

Under most conditions, semitransparent stain has a shorter life span than either paint or solid-color stain.

Water sealer. Applied to unfinished wood, clear sealers won't color the wood but will darken it slightly. You can buy them in oil- or water-based

versions. Many formulations include both UV-blockers and mildewcides to protect wood; some come in slightly tinted versions. Like semitransparent stains, sealers need to be renewed every few years, but they allow you to show off wood that has a beautiful grain and color.

Set into a hillside, this cottage built of rustic stone and roofed with wood shakes has become an almost integral element in the landscape.

Some masonry materials, such as stucco, are applied to wood framing and sheathing. Others, like true adobe or rammed earth, actually form the walls.

OTHER CHOICES. *Vinyl and aluminum sidings,* with factory-applied enamel coating in a variety of colors and textures, mimic the look of horizontal board siding. They are generally durable and low-maintenance, although some vinyl siding can become stiff and crack in extreme cold. *Corrugated aluminum sheet siding* is sometimes used to convey an up-to-date industrial look.

Walls of *safety glass or plastic*— nowadays, usually clear polycarbonate— let in maximum sunlight and trap heat inside; venting is important to prevent moisture buildup.

Yet another possibility is the traditional *log cabin* with the logs forming the walls and no additional siding applied.

MASONRY. A completely different look is presented by homes constructed of *stucco* (often associated with Mediterranean or Spanish architecture), *stone* (rustic and natural), *brick* (new or old), *cement block,* or *adobe* (a mixture of sand, clay, water, and sometimes straw). New, environmentally friendly techniques developed for building with rammed or cast earth or straw bales result in houses that have the look of adobe.

FOOLING THE EYE

One creative way to dress up the wall of a shed or cottage is to fool the eye with *trompe l'oeil* painting. An entire scene or a fragment of one can bring a Parisian street corner to your backyard or create a blooming vine on a wall where in reality nothing will grow.

Using shadowing and perspective, trompe l'oeil gives the illusion of three dimensions. The painted scene can even be cleverly mixed with actual objects—a real pot of flowers hanging on the painted wall, for example.

Painters who achieve such effects can be found through interior decorators and paint stores. Ask to see the artist's portfolio or, if possible, on-site work.

A contemporary summerhouse makes its design statement via elegant leaded-glass French doors and casement windows on all sides.

Additional embellishments help set your style. Windows may be flanked by shutters, overhung with awnings, or underscored with window boxes. Doors may sport decorative hardware and other ornaments. And don't overlook the effect of curtains or shades when viewed from outside.

If insects—or larger critters—are a potential problem, you may want to install screen doors and windows that accept screens.

DOOR CHOICES. Doors suitable for backyard cottages may be basic exterior wood doors (with or without glass windows), patio doors (French or sliding), Dutch doors (with independent upper and lower sections), barn doors on overhead tracks, or roll-up garage-style doors.

Will your structure be used for storage of garden equipment or large items? Calculate whether you might need an extra-wide, double, or garage-style door to facilitate moving large items in and out.

Windows and doors

You can select new windows and doors in a variety of standard sizes, shapes, and materials from specialty manufacturers, home improvement centers, or lumberyards. Recycled windows and doors offer another possibility; just keep in mind that extra attention must be paid to fitting your finds into new construction and making them weathertight.

The way you finish your windows and doors will go a long way toward setting your cottage style. A rustic unfinished Dutch door creates one impression, a door with a bright coat of high-gloss paint another. Similarly, window frames may be natural-finish wood or colorfully painted. Consider whether you want your window and door frames to blend into the total picture or to stand out as decorative elements in themselves.

ENERGY-EFFICIENT WINDOWS

Most windows are rated with a "U value" to indicate the rate of heat flow through them. The lower the U value, the more energy-efficient the window; a low value (0.2 to 0.3) is preferable in a cold climate, while an average U value (0.4 to 0.6) is fine in a warm climate. Look for the rating on the manufacturer's label. In general, old-fashioned double-hung windows tend to have higher

U values than casement and awning windows, which seal better.

Double-glazing, or insulating glass made of two panes of glass sealed together with space between, can go a long way toward preventing heat loss. The newer low-e (low-emissivity) glass adds a coating that reduces indoor heat loss in cold weather and keeps ultraviolet rays out—which helps prevent fading of

furnishings. Tinted glass can also block solar heat gain to help keep your cottage cool in hot weather.

Don't overlook the old-fashioned canvas awning or the vine-covered "eyebrow" or overhead trellis—naturals for keeping out hot sun. In addition, caulking and weather-stripping doors and windows is an easy, inexpensive way to increase energy efficiency.

WINDOW OPTIONS. Windows come in almost unlimited shapes, or you can gang various shapes and sizes to create a window wall. Most basic shapes are available as standard orders from home improvement centers or companies that specialize in windows, or you can custom-order special shapes, sizes, and kinds of glass—at a price, of course.

Besides regular window glass, you can choose decorative treatments such as beveled glass, stained glass, diamond-pane windows, bull's-eyes or roundels (resembling the bottoms of glass bottles), or contemporary-looking glass block (see photo on page 98).

Frames may be of wood, wood with aluminum or vinyl cladding, aluminum, vinyl, steel, or fiberglass. Wood has the advantage of being paintable in any color, but cladding (available in a range of colors) eliminates most exterior maintenance problems. Aluminum—the least expensive alternative—is low-maintenance but stylistically more limited. Vinyl is virtually maintenance-free, though it lacks the natural feel and look of wood; fiberglass is similar but varies in quality. Durable steel, the most expensive choice, is excellent for clean, contemporary styling. Aluminum and steel windows generally do not insulate as well as other types.

SKYLIGHTS. Available in a wide range of sizes and styles, fixed and operable, with or without screens, a skylight may be the answer if you have privacy issues or want extra light and ventilation. Consider placement carefully; a south-facing skylight can offer dramatic shifting light throughout the day but may let in too much light and heat, whereas a north-facing skylight usually provides soft, uniform light rather than high drama.

WINDOWS DEFINED

Windows can be operable or fixed, or you can combine the two—a fixed square window directly above or below an awning window, for example. Here is a brief survey of the types most commonly used for cottages.

Awning. A good choice because of its small size and simplicity, this window is hinged on top to open out from the bottom; when open, it acts like an awning to keep out rain.

Casement. Hinged on one side to be cranked or pushed open, this style provides maximum ventilation—and the tight seals on today's casement windows make them especially energy-efficient.

Clerestory. Usually small and fixed, these high windows let in light while maintaining privacy. Practical only in buildings with relatively high ceilings, they can be useful in a larger cottage where privacy is an issue.

Decorative. Small decorative windows may be round—called *ox-eye*—as well as hexagonal, triangular, or other shapes; they're usually fixed rather than operable.

Double-hung. This traditional window has upper and lower sashes that slide up and down by means of springs, weights, or friction devices. With or without divided glass panes, it gives any dwelling a classic look.

Picture. This large fixed pane of glass, sometimes flanked by operable windows, might be considered to emphasize an expansive view. Otherwise, it's less appropriate in scale than other windows for most cottages.

Sliding-sash. This window moves horizontally, like a sliding Japanese screen, in grooves or between runners at the top and bottom of the window frame.

CASEMENT (TOP RIGHT)

DOUBLE-HUNG (MIDDLE RIGHT)

AWNING (BOTTOM RIGHT)

OCTAGONAL (ABOVE)

The "fun" elements of a cottage exterior can take many forms. Fanciful trim plus vines espaliered in decorative patterns dress up a wood-frame cottage (top); an ornate porch railing makes a charming focal point (above); decorative timber brackets add interest to the gable end of a backyard studio (right).

Trim and embellishments

Here's the fun part of cottage building—the opportunity to put a personal stamp on your backyard creation. You can take the most basic structure, be it a revamped garage or a shed built from a kit, and give it color, life, and individuality by adding your own decorative details.

Elements like rafters, trim, and such embellishments as cupolas are integral to a building. (The practical purpose of trim is to cover or protect joints, edges, or ends of siding or other materials.) Over the centuries, architectural styles have been defined as much by their trim—or lack of it—as by their general forms. One obvious example is the highly decorative woodwork associated with the Victorian "gingerbread" style.

The hardware on your cottage—doorknobs, hinges, and so on—provides another opportunity for expression. While hardware can be purely functional and almost invisible, it can also be decorative and even whimsical.

Unlike integral decorations, a host of purely decorative objects—signs, objets d'art, and other ornaments—can be tacked onto cottage walls with a hammer and nails.

Here are a few ideas for adding decorative touches to your cottage exterior:

- Decorative tiles on walls, across steps, around windows or doors—grouted in or hung on hooks
- Signs, plaques, and small art pieces, hung singly or in groups
- Lattices and trellises, fixed to the cottage or anchored in large pots or planting boxes set against the walls
- Lanterns or sconces, decorative or functional
- Mirrors on exterior walls
- Window and door shutters, working or strictly decorative
- Baskets and buckets hung on walls or set on a porch
- Antique tools or other objects mounted on walls in rows or patterns

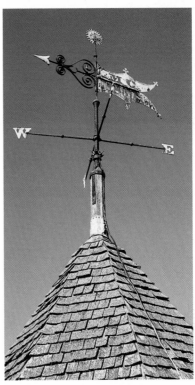

It's all in the details: a sign and found objects personalize a gardener's shed (left), a weathervane tops a steeply pitched roof (above), and a garden trowel becomes a door handle (top).

Beautiful Surroundings

ENHANCING YOUR COTTAGE'S APPEAL WITH ARTFUL LANDSCAPING

What could be more appealing than a cottage set at the end of a curving garden path, nestled among the trees as if it's always been there—or at the edge of a backyard patio, knee-deep in a bed of flowers? Whatever its size and style, your backyard cottage is part and parcel of a larger picture that includes your private landscape (your yard and garden), your main house, and perhaps even your neighborhood. Ideally, everything should blend harmoniously.

How you incorporate your backyard structure into your landscape is partly governed by the size of your property. A large lot obviously gives you the widest range of options: you can tuck a cottage or shed out of sight among the trees, place it as a focal point to be viewed across a rolling green lawn or even a pond, or incorporate it into a more formal complex that includes house, patio, garden beds, and perhaps a swimming pool. On a smaller lot, your challenge is to integrate the cottage into the landscape while keeping it in proportion to the property and garden as a whole.

This cottage courtyard has it all—a fountain splashes gently; container plantings clamber up walls and bloom in corners; and brick paving, tiled stucco walls, and rustic wood accents create no-fuss style.

Landscape features are generally divided into "hardscape" (pathways, patios, decks, fences, and walls) and plantings. Both can play a role in connecting your cottage to the main house and creating a pleasing outdoor environment.

Pathways, patios, and decks

Patios and decks form the "floor" of your landscape, while pathways are like hallways—they connect your cot-

tage with your house and with the rest of your property.

PATIOS AND DECKS. Outdoor "floors" may surround your cottage or be situated on just one or two sides. They can function as extensions of your cottage, expanding perceived and actual usable space. In good weather, a patio or deck can be a dining room, a sunroom—even a dance floor!

You may be able to design a landscape in which the patio is a widening of the path to your cottage, with both made of the same materials. The deck or patio itself need not be a square or rectangle; curved and irregular shapes are graceful and can accommodate unusual property configurations.

Generally, patios are installed on flat sites, whereas wood decks, which usually rest on vertical posts set in concrete, have the flexibility to span sloping ground. Decks are usually built of decay-resistant woods such as redwood or cedar, of pressure-treated lumber, or of the newer, environmentally friendly wood products such as synthetic wood-polymer composites. Patios, like paths, can be constructed of a variety of materials. Proper grading and preparation of the bed on which a patio surface will be installed are essential; consult your supplier for details, or see the Sunset book *Ideas for Great Patios & Decks*.

PATHWAYS. A path might be straight and true, leading directly from, say, the back patio of your main house to your cottage; or it might meander in curves through your property.

Straight paths could be flanked by beds of flowers or by low hedges. Such paths—and geometric or symmetrical garden layouts—usually convey an air of formality. A quite different feeling is created by a path that is winding and enshrouded by plantings so that its destination isn't obvious at first, allowing visitors to "discover" the cottage at path's end.

Any path, straight or meandering, will be most comfortable for walking if it is at least 4 feet wide.

Walls, fences, and overheads

Perhaps your backyard cottage is uncomfortably close to the neighbors, or maybe you want a sense of enclosure even if privacy isn't an issue. Or perhaps

PATH AND PATIO PAVINGS

Choices in path and patio surfaces abound; each has its own particular look as well as practical attributes.

Bark and chips. Shredded bark, wood chips, and other loose materials are soft and springy, inexpensive, and easy to install (they do require a header or edging to contain them). They drain well and create a casual look. Clearing off fallen leaves can be difficult, because the bark tends to get raked up with the leaves.

Brick. Classic brick pavers can be set in a variety of patterns, in sand or in mortar. Mortar-set bricks can give a formal or contemporary look, while bricks in sand tend to look more casual, less uniform. A mortared surface is smoother and easier to maintain, but sand affords better drainage. Either surface can be slippery when wet.

Concrete. As a poured slab or individual pavers, concrete is durable and versatile. You can have poured concrete in a host of tints and textures, stamped to look like stone tile or flagstone, or in irregularly shaped pads with planting spaces between.

Individual square pavers, laid in sand, can be butted together or separated by gravel or a ground cover. Or you can choose circles, rectangles, irregular shapes, or interlocking pavers (see examples on facing page). Inexpensive and simple to use, most concrete pavers are ideal for do-it-yourselfers.

Gravel. Available in a variety of textures and tones (white and red as well as grays), gravel can be raked into patterns or used as a decorative element with other paving materials. It must be confined inside edgings or headers.

Relatively inexpensive and quick-draining, gravel does have two drawbacks: it can be hard to keep clear of fallen leaves, and it can scratch flooring when tracked indoors.

Stone. Durable and beautiful, stone has timeless appeal. Natural flagstones or cut tiles come in a wide range of subtle colors and textures (see examples below right). This is one of the more expensive paving options, though cost varies according to where you live in relation to where the stone originates.

Stones thicker than about 1 inch can be set in sand, with gravel or plantings in between; with time they will settle into the garden almost as if nature had placed them there. Thinner stones need to be set in mortar, resulting in a smoother surface with a more formal look.

Some stone can be slippery when wet, and some porous types stain easily.

Tile. Ceramic paving tiles in natural-colored terra-cotta or brightly colored patterns can add style and beauty to any patio. The stablest bed for outdoor tile is mortar over a concrete slab, though sometimes heavy tiles can be laid in sand; ask your supplier. Glazed tiles are extremely slippery when wet; unglazed tiles are best for paths and patios, with perhaps a few fancy glazed ones as accents. If you live in a cold climate, select tile that is freeze-thaw stable, identified as impervious or vitreous.

Tile should be sealed for protection against surface water and stains; if your tile isn't factory sealed, ask your supplier for recommendations.

Certain elements—a white picket fence paired with a perennial border, a rose-covered arbor entrance—are classic expressions of cottage charm.

you want to visually define the boundaries of an area around your cottage. A fence or wall—one constructed of wood or masonry or a "living" fence of foliage—may be just what you need.

You may have a situation like that shown on pages 34–35, with a cottage near the property line benefiting from a fairly high fence. Or you may have a setting in which a private courtyard could extend a cottage's livable space. For just the suggestion of a boundary, you may simply want to partially surround your structure with something low and open—an old-fashioned picket fence, perhaps, or a split-rail or Japanese tied-bamboo fence.

As with any structure you build on your property, you will need to consult local zoning and building codes (see pages 20–21).

In choosing materials, consider the look and style of the structures on your property. Usually it's best to match or at least coordinate materials for a unified look. And don't overlook the softening effect of vines; they can add an attractive layer of color and texture. In fact, often you can save money by using less solid barriers such as lattice panels or wood-and-wire fencing in combination with climbing plants to achieve privacy and a sense of separation.

Of course, you can also use plants alone. Trees, shrubs, or even bamboo (where its roots can be controlled) can make terrific screens, though they will take time to become established.

To create a garden "room" adjacent to your backyard cottage or to extend its roofed area, consider adding an overhead in the form of an arbor, either freestanding or attached to the cottage wall or roof. In addition to offering a frame for flowering or leafy plantings, an arbor adds a pleasing vertical dimension to the landscape and provides filtered shade where needed. Sometimes a small arbor—with or without an attached fence and gate—can be used to create an entry area in front of a cottage.

This welcoming entrance to a cottage courtyard is distinguished by a simple overhead structure that can support climbing vines.

Plantings

Unless you're landscaping your property from scratch, you'll probably be fitting your cottage into a landscape that already features established trees, shrubs, and planting beds. You'll need to decide what you want to keep and what you want to modify or add to the present garden.

If you want a clean, open look that emphasizes the building and makes it appear larger, you might opt for paving the area around your cottage, then adding a narrow strip of foundation plantings, container plants, or a combination.

For the opposite effect, and to give the cottage a settled-in look, surround it closely with lush, massed plantings. Trees and shrubs immediately surrounding the cottage will tend to make it appear smaller and less dominating in your landscape. Foundation plantings or many containers massed close to the foundation will help anchor your cottage to the site. A double row of plantings (taller ones in back) will create a sense of depth; in fact, layering plants is one surefire way to create depth on a small lot.

If you have a tight space that does not allow for much in-ground planting, or if you want to enhance and soften your cottage's appearance, wood or metal trellises can be placed against walls, around windows, and over doorways to encourage leafy and flowering vines to clamber up the sides and even over the roof. The vines can be planted in the ground at the base of the walls or in containers.

Handcrafted low-voltage copper lanterns light a garden path (right). A decorative garden lantern of cast metal can hold a candle (far right).

In addition, you might consider installing window boxes and filling them with flowers as well as spilling and trailing plants. Or you can add color and greenery in pots attached to walls with metal hangers and in hanging pots suspended from eaves or overhangs.

Any new trees and shrubs that you plant should be appropriately scaled to the size of your cottage. Be sure to check how tall and wide they will eventually grow.

Outdoor lighting

If you plan to use your garden and cottage at night, you'll need to light the way to it. Landscape lighting is an art in itself, transforming outdoor spaces into magical and often dramatic scenes as well as addressing safety concerns.

Lighting pathways is a must, and many low-voltage systems now available feature fixtures designed to be placed at intervals along paths. You can purchase kits to install yourself or have a system custom-designed and installed. In addition, lights mounted on

A Southwest-style courtyard gives an impression of lavish color and pattern, thanks to containers brimming with blooms.

trees and on cottage or house walls and eaves can cast light down onto steps and paths, while strategically positioned upward-facing lights can be used to dramatically illuminate trees and shrubbery. For an easy and delightful addition to permanent lighting, use strings of mini-lights along steps, railings, and walkways. Other decorative lighting can include hanging or wall-mounted lanterns.

Ask at your local home improvement center, lighting store, or hardware store for information about specific outdoor lighting needs. For a professional-quality overall lighting plan, consult a lighting designer.

Inside Story

FLOOR, WALL, AND WINDOW TREATMENTS CREATE ATMOSPHERE AND STYLE

The interior of your cottage may be plain or fancy, sparely furnished or filled with friendly clutter. The way you will use your cottage and its basic construction style are the two factors that most affect how you "do" its indoor space.

A rustic structure that's partly open to the elements will most likely be one you'll furnish simply—with minimal decoration and with wall and floor treatments and furniture that can withstand exposure to temperature variations, even blowing rain or snow. A working potting shed or a sculpture studio calls for unfussy flooring and wall treatments that can take some hard knocks. At the other end of the spectrum, a house-in-miniature guest cottage allows you to pull out all the stops when it comes to flooring and wall treatments, furnishings and decorative elements.

Consider the role that textures play in setting a tone. Rough wood or stone, nubby fabrics, and earthenware or basketry tend to give a rustic, comfortable feeling. Smooth, finished textures—polished wood or metal, some ceramic tile, glass or acrylic, and silky fabrics—convey an air of refinement and perhaps modernity. (Of course, you will mix these elements to some extent, and that can add interest to any interior.)

Color, too, plays an important role. Natural wood tones are often associated with warmth and coziness. White or soft pastels can give a room a light, airy, or romantic feeling; bright primary colors liven up the atmosphere instantly. One versatile approach is to let walls and flooring be fairly neutral, or natural wood, and add interest with color accents—on woodwork or in decorative accessories.

Flooring

Even in a fully furnished guest cottage, flooring should be of practical, long-wearing material that demands little upkeep and can withstand comings and goings from pool, garden, or patio. Generally, it's wise to stay away from wall-to-wall carpeting, which can suffer from dampness in a cottage that sits unheated for periods of time and can be hard to keep clean. If soft floor coverings are called for, choose area rugs and smaller throw rugs—perhaps hooked or braided rugs or matting such as seagrass or sisal.

Cottage flooring can be light and fanciful, like the painted wood at top, or elegant and enduring, like the slate tiles above. At left are examples of unglazed terra-cotta floor tiles and decorative glazed tiles.

FLOORING SAMPLER

Here's a guide to flooring choices that are both practical and attractive for a back-yard cottage.

CERAMIC TILE

Ceramic tile. A practical choice, ceramic tile is available in a vast array of colors and patterns. For a rustic look, you can choose unglazed quarry or terra-cotta tiles (be aware that these are porous and can get stained unless properly sealed). Rough, water-resistant red-clay tiles, rugged, stone-like porcelain pavers, and glazed floor tiles are all good choices but can be slippery when wet.

STONE WITH MOSAIC TILE INSET

Stone tile. Natural stone (such as slate or limestone) cut into tiles makes beautiful and durable flooring that's especially attractive in a building that has close connections with the outdoors. Although the cost can be high, stone is long-lasting and classic in design.

Concrete. No longer confined to slabs of gray, concrete flooring can now look stylish and interesting, thanks to tinting and etching techniques that give it color and pattern. Although a bare concrete floor can be cold underfoot, it's also extremely durable and easy to care for—and you can always add area rugs to warm it up. Of course, a plain concrete slab can also be the base for almost any other kind of flooring.

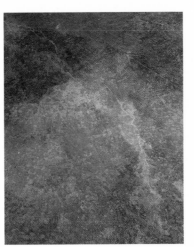

TINTED CONCRETE

Brick. Suitable for on-grade structures that have no raised foundations, such as potting sheds and rustic retreats, brick is durable and can be either laid in sand or installed with mortared joints.

Wood. A classic hardwood floor is hard to beat for warmth, versatility, and good looks. If your cottage has a raised floor (subflooring laid over wood joists), you can nail wood flooring onto the subfloor. If you're on a concrete slab foundation that's level and in good condition, you can install a "floating" floor of

RED FIR

prefinished wood veneer or one of the plastic laminates that looks like wood.

Hardwood floors can be sanded and refinished as they age; prefinished floors are particularly durable, and the thicker veneers can be sanded and refinished once or twice. Some creative souls have used vintage recycled wood flooring with success; its mellow character is unrivaled.

Resilient flooring. A low-maintenance, practical choice, this category includes solid vinyl or polyurethane sheet flooring or tiles and old-fashioned linoleum and cork—natural products available with updated looks.

LINOLEUM

cottage elements

WARMING UP

Unless you live in a tropical climate, your winter weather probably ranges from chilly and damp to freezing cold. To use your backyard cottage during the cold months, you'll need some kind of insulation and heating.

If you are building a new structure, you have the opportunity to add insulation in the ceiling (the most important), in the walls, and—if there's a raised floor rather than, say, an on-grade concrete slab—under the flooring. Your architect or contractor can advise you about what kind of insulation to use.

You can also raise the temperature inside your cottage by choosing the right windows—preferably insulating double-glazed ones as described on page 104. South-facing windows and skylights will make the most of the sun's warmth during the day. A tile, concrete, or brick floor warmed by the sun can act as passive solar heating as it absorbs warmth and radiates it back.

As for heating, you have several options. While gas heat is the most efficient, you'll need to have a gas line run to your cottage—practical only for a fairly large-scale project. A delightful and practical option is a wood stove, now available in a wide range of styles and sizes; new models, including pellet-burning stoves, are designed to burn fuel cleanly. Check with your local building department to find out if a stove is permissible and how it must be installed. Consult local dealers and Internet web sites for general information about wood stoves.

The easiest option of all is a plug-in electric heater such as the radiator types widely available. Although electric heating is expensive, it's an instant way to make your space toasty—but check with your local utility company or consult an electrician to make sure the power supply to your cottage is adequate to handle the demands of a plug-in heater.

A wood stove warms this cozy space; thick cast-earth walls provide extra insulation as well as sculptured good looks.

Creative ways with paint and stenciling— including a stenciled message above the windows—make this cottage interior a delight.

Wall treatments

Unless you have a rustic structure with interior walls left unfinished (like the one shown on page 98), the walls of your cottage will probably be finished with wood paneling or sheetrock nailed onto the wall studs.

Wood paneling can be either solid-board or sheet paneling. Generally, solid boards have edges specially milled to overlap or interlock. They may be narrow tongue-and-groove (a quintessential vintage cottage look), or wider boards installed vertically or horizontally. As with flooring, a handy builder can recycle vintage interior paneling to create walls with a unique aged beauty.

Sheet paneling is a catchall term for wall paneling that comes in large, machine-made panels; it's less expensive than solid board paneling but less durable, and it doesn't have the same classic good looks.

Good-quality solid-board paneling may be left natural (unfinished) and sealed, or be stained and sealed. In fact, wood paneling such as knotty pine is practically synonymous with cabin and cottage style. Wood paneling of any type can also be painted, of course—as can sheetrock. Latex paint in flat, eggshell, and satin finishes is available in every color of the rainbow, premixed or custom-mixed. Preselected coordinated palettes for walls, ceilings, and trim are sometimes offered by paint companies. But remember that out in your backyard cottage you have the freedom to exercise your imagination and creativity without making the same level of commitment to style and formality that your main house might require.

Particularly popular today are faux paint finishes that feature techniques such as pickling, sponging, ragging, and color washing. These can be used to create all kinds of effects, from the illusion of an antique, peeling surface to a wall that glows with rich layers of subtly mixed colors. For more information about faux finishes, see the Sunset book *Decorative Paint & Faux Finishes*. Other decorative ways with paint, such as stenciling or trompe l'oeil painting (see page 103), are a wonderful way to dress up your space and put a personal stamp on its decor.

Generally speaking, wallpaper is less practical for a backyard structure—unless it's a fairly elaborate, heated cottage. Wallpaper is subject to mildew when dampness is present, and, except for the wipeable vinyl type, it's vulnerable to dirt. It usually requires an even wall surface for proper installation.

Artful stenciling (top left) can transform a simple architectural element into a focal point. Old-fashioned beadboard gains panache with a faux-painting process known as pickling (top right), while solid board paneling takes on a whole new look when applied horizontally and washed with a striking stain (left). Below, traditional knotty-pine paneling looks clean and contemporary around a tiled zero-clearance fireplace.

Window treatments

If your cottage is in a secluded setting, or if you're using it for entertaining or other pursuits that don't require privacy, it's often best to leave windows uncovered—the better to admit sunlight and garden views. Style-wise, many windows are so attractive in their own right that it's a shame to cover them up.

But if privacy is an issue, if windows feel bare or cold, or if you will be using your cottage at night and don't want the "black hole" effect of uncovered windows, you will want window treatments that complement and carry out the style of your cottage. Most backyard cottages call for something fairly casual and unstructured rather than formal draperies or fancy shades. But here again, your cottage is the place to indulge your stylistic whims and fantasies—and if that calls for elegant balloon shades or Victorian velvet drapes, so be it.

Most window treatments fall into two main categories: "soft" treatments such as curtains and fabric shades, and "hard" treatments such as shutters and blinds. The following is a brief survey of options.

CURTAINS. Fabric curtains are the most versatile and may be the least expensive choice. Informal curtains can be gathered on a rod or attached to a rod by tabs, rings, or ties. They can be made

to any length, either with or without a valance—an abbreviated "curtain" at the top of a window. Or you can opt for unstructured swags of fabric simply draped around the window frame.

The range of fabrics available allows you to vary the look, from country-style gingham to romantic gauze. If you like to sew, you can whip up simple curtains in a jiffy; other options include having them custom-made or buying ready-made curtains from home furnishing stores, specialty shops, and mail-order or Internet outlets.

Seen from the outside, an inexpensive bamboo shade contributes casual good looks to a cottage window as well as providing daytime privacy.

Washable curtains are most practical in a cottage subject to mildew from dampness or temperature extremes.

Hardware for curtains—rods, finials, and holdbacks—is available in many styles and materials. These elements can help set the style of your cottage interior.

SHADES. One popular and practical choice for a backyard cottage is the familiar bamboo shade, along with its cousins made of woven natural grasses and reeds. You can choose anything from inexpensive roll-ups from import stores to custom-made woven shades.

Among fabric shades, the simpler, tailored types—such as roller and Roman shades or the contemporary honeycomb type—are generally the most appropriate for a cottage. These can be made up in almost as wide a variety of fabrics as can curtains—even canvas or special indoor-outdoor fabrics. Some types—especially the newer pleated shades with an insulating honeycomb design—help to conserve energy.

Shades may be lined or unlined. Again, you can make them yourself (see

Curtain rod finials and holdbacks in floral or abstract designs add that extra decorative touch to cottage window treatments.

the Sunset book *Simply Window Treatments*) or have them custom-made. If dampness and mildew are an issue, keep in mind that fabric shades can be more difficult to take down than curtains, and most require dry-cleaning.

SHUTTERS AND SCREENS.
Louvered wood or wood-look interior shutters are unrivaled for durability and style. Available in natural-finish wood, painted, or unpainted (for you to finish), they can be found with the traditional 1¼-inch louvers or with wider louvers ("plantation shutters"). While shutters are one of the more expensive window treatment options, with good care they will look attractive for years. You may be able to find ready-made shutters to fit your windows (the least costly); otherwise, you'll need to have them made.

One interesting option is the traditional Japanese shoji screen, which features a wood frame with a special paper or fiberglass insert that lets soft light enter the room while maintaining privacy. Shoji screens may either slide in a track or be hinged to fold open like shutters.

BLINDS. This "hard" window treatment is perfect in a cottage with a contemporary look, whether you choose traditional Venetian blinds with 2-inch slats or miniblinds with 1-inch slats. Blinds can be wood, painted aluminum, or polycarbonate plastic, in a rainbow of colors and patterns; Venetion blinds also come with fabric slats. Blinds are a practical choice when you want clean good looks along with privacy and light control.

A graceful fabric swag (top left) is all you need to dress up a window that looks out on a pretty view; ruffle-trimmed cotton curtains with simple tiebacks say "country cabin" (top right); for a tailored, contemporary treatment, choose miniblinds (above).

Feathering the Nest

SPACE-SAVING FURNISHINGS, STORAGE IDEAS, AND LIGHTING

Almost by definition, space in a backyard cottage is at a premium. That miniaturized quality is part of the charm of such a structure, but if you also want the space to feel comfortably cozy without being crowded—and if you have things you need to store in your cottage—it's important to use your space efficiently.

Try to suit the scale and amount of furnishings and accessories to both the scale and the function of your cottage. For example, a tiny reading retreat may need only a chair or two and perhaps a bookshelf and some plants— much more would ruin its atmosphere of repose. A potting shed, on the other hand, is meant for storage as well as work—and sometimes it's also a place to sit and relax. It may feature shelving and bins, a work surface that can double as storage, and perhaps a chair or bench. At the other end of the spectrum, a guest cottage might include sleeping, dining, and food preparation areas, all on a small scale. Here, clever use must be made of space to provide for sleeping, seating, and storage.

Storage units and space-saving, multipurpose furniture will be your best tools for creating a workable, livable space. For storage pieces, visit specialty storage stores, home improvement

The friendly clutter of a working artist's private space speaks volumes about the owner's interests and passions. Every surface is used for display, from windowsills and high ledges to countertops and the shelves beneath them.

A quilter's idea of heaven might be an at-a-glance display like this one, which groups fabrics by color in a generous system of built-in shelves.

Supplementing shelves and bins in a potting shed, a wire grid with S hooks makes a handy storage wall that also shows off favorite objects. (For more views of this space, see pages 44–45.)

centers, and even hardware stores, and study catalogs—there's lots to choose from! For space-saving furniture, look at home furnishing catalogs and magazines, especially those that feature living in small spaces.

In plain sight

In the small, casual setting of a backyard cottage, storing things in plain sight helps conserve space and contributes to a lived-in feeling. Here are a few ideas for doing so in an attractive, organized way. Be sure that anything mounted on the wall is firmly anchored, preferably on a backing board that is screwed into the wall studs.

OPEN SHELVING. Fasten wood, wire, coated-wire, or glass shelving to the walls—use traditional shelves with brackets or the newer, keyhole-mounted "floating" shelves. Or purchase small wall-hung drawer units, display cupboards, or racks.

If you have exposed studs in unfinished walls, install shelves between the studs to take advantage of the space. (Recessed shelving and wall niches are also constructed this way, but the framing is usually hidden behind the sheetrock or paneling.) Of course, you can always make use of modular freestanding units.

A roll-around shelf unit backed with fabric-covered panels stores and displays things wherever you want them at the moment.

STACKING BINS AND BASKETS. You can purchase sets or mix and match components, or you can buy individual plastic or metal bins or wicker baskets to organize items on a bookshelf or other ready-made shelving unit. For maximum flexibility, consider units that can be rolled around.

PEG RACKS AND HOOKS. For a quick and easy storage solution, mount a Shaker wooden peg rack or a row of coat hooks—or even vintage doorknobs—along a wall to hang just about anything: jackets and hats, gardener's tote bags, even (as the Shakers did) ladder-back chairs. Or mount a curtain rod along a wall at waist height or above a work counter to hang items individually or in baskets or canvas bags, using the kind of hooks designed for pot racks.

A classic cottage entryway features a row of hooks on which to sling jackets, hats, and bags; a bench beneath provides a place to sit and pull off boots. Baskets, lined (like those below) or unlined, are available at stores specializing in storage; use them alone or tuck them into shelves.

Good old Peg-Board is a practical, inexpensive, and good-looking "canvas" for storing and displaying everything from garden tools to cooking utensils. Paint it for a dressier look.

PEG-BOARD AND GRIDS. Traditionally the handyman's best friend, a perforated storage surface takes up almost no room and is both inexpensive and practical; for a more finished look, you can paint the board. Both perforated-board and wire-grid systems accept a variety of hooks, brackets for small shelves, and little bins or drawers.

LEDGES. Whether they are part of your cottage's construction (as shown on page 51) or added later, ledges running around your walls are great places to park small items, both useful and decorative.

Display pretty seeds, pebbles, or other treasures in jars; hang objects you love to look at, like these watering cans, on a row of hooks.

Carefully designed built-in furniture can do more than double duty. Beneath this couch are pull-out storage compartments, and a low bookcase extends from one end. The cushion is mattress-size, providing a spare bed.

Clever furnishings

Furnishing a small space gives you the opportunity to use your creativity and imagination. Here are a few ideas for compact approaches to using furniture.
VINTAGE AND VINTAGE-STYLE. Don't overlook such pieces as armoires, Hoosier cabinets, wash-stands, buffets, hutches, and chests that can make great storage and work areas. You can even convert an armoire into a self-contained "mini-office," sewing center, or potting workbench by modifying its interior with hooks, additional shelves, and so on.

Older furniture doesn't have to be in perfect shape; in fact, you can create a wonderful one-of-a-kind piece with creative use of paint and such decorative techniques as stenciling.

Updated with a contemporary plumbed-in sink and faucet, an antique washstand is now a compact, all-in-one vanity, sink, and towel rack.

Cabinets, countertops, drawers, and shelving offer storage and work space galore in this fabric artist's garage-size studio. You can create a space like this with ready-made cabinets and countertops.

A *built-in system of shelf, counter, and storage cubes is handsome as well as practical. Shelf molding and board paneling, as well as framed botanical prints, plants, and decorative bric-a-brac, lend style to this hard-working arrangement.*

BUILT-IN. Time-honored built-ins like Murphy beds that fold down from the wall, benches with lids that lift to reveal storage compartments, and built-in buffet/china cabinets are being updated in keeping with today's trend toward smaller houses. If you are handy yourself or can afford to hire a carpenter, you can equip your cottage with built-in furniture that fulfills several functions at once.

Handcrafted for a tiny guest house, a pull-out table allows a custom wall unit to double as a surface for working, eating, or serving. The 22-inch-deep tabletop retracts into a bookcase.

A drawer built under a window seat provides clever camouflaged storage for files in a small-space cottage office.

Ample windows above a cottage sink bathe the room in natural light during the daytime; soft recessed lighting and track lights turn up the wattage when natural light wanes.

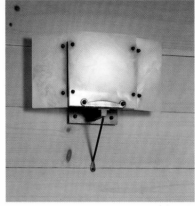

A contemporary wall fixture is a work of art as well as a source of light.

Part of the charm of a simple cottage without electricity is the cozy, camping-out atmosphere created by the flickering light of candles and lanterns. (Just be sure to use them safely and to never leave them unattended.) If your cottage does have wiring, you may use anything from simple table lamps to beautiful wired-in ceiling and wall fixtures.

For the most effective lighting, use a combination of *ambient lighting* (soft light from overhead sources) and *task and accent lighting* (track lights and freestanding lamps that focus light for reading and other pursuits or that illuminate objects for display).

Indoor lighting

By day, natural light is often all you need to brighten your cottage. Leave a French door open so light and air stream in; leave windows (especially south-facing ones) uncurtained to admit maximum sunlight. On overcast days or in a cottage that doesn't receive bright light, supplement natural light with light fixtures. And if you will be using your cottage at night, of course you'll need to plan for some form of lighting. Light fixtures can do much to set the style of your cottage decor.

The soft glow of an old-fashioned oil lamp (left) or a contemporary electric lamp like the one at right, with a rustic twig base, should inspire convivial evenings in any backyard cottage.

Decorative touches

Whether you've built your dream cottage from the ground up or are dressing up an existing shed, adding your own touches will give your backyard getaway a unique personal style. It's with these details that you really get to have fun—in large part because this is a private, informal environment where anything goes.

You can go for a particular style you love—be it classic American country, tropical island, or French Provençal—and assemble everything in keeping with that style, from curtains to drinking glasses. You can focus on a color scheme—all white, perhaps, or brilliant primaries—and carry it out with

American folk art objects like this birdhouse make lighthearted accents. Below, quilts add cheery color to fresh white basics.

Gather flowers from your own garden to bring brightness and fragrance into your cottage.

It's all in how you look at it; why not use a stepladder as a display rack?

If you own dishes you love, you needn't hide them away in cabinets. Displayed on open shelves, they can become part of your cottage decor.

vases of flowers, baskets, fabrics, lampshades, even knickknacks. Or you can simply fill your cottage with everything you love—vintage gardening tools, botanical prints bought on a trip to Europe, or all those mismatched fabric samples you've been collecting, sewn into a delightful hodgepodge of throw pillows for a built-in bench.

Think of your cottage's wall, floor, and window treatments as a backdrop for your "gallery" of beloved things. Hang prints and posters, mirrors, interesting signs, quilts, and related decorative objects or plates arranged in interesting patterns. Line up pretty bottles, dishes and cups, figurines, small potted plants or vases of flowers, and other small objects on shelves, ledges, and windowsills. Hang baskets or even antique tools from rafters.

Grouping art pieces like these colorful hand-painted "calendar" plaques, can have a big design impact.

PROJECT PLANS

A BACKYARD COTTAGE is a welcome addition to any home. If the ideas you've seen in this book have inspired you, check out the plans for sale on the following pages. Whether you're looking for a tiny playhouse or a full-size guest cottage, you'll find a variety of options. And if you build it yourself, you'll have the added satisfaction of watching the structure take shape with each saw cut and swing of the hammer. ALL THE ORDERING INFORMATION you'll need is provided on the opposite page. Just choose the plan that's right for you beginning on page 128 and call, fax, or mail in your order. Soon you'll be well on your way to an exciting new addition to your backyard.

IMPORTANT INFORMATION TO KNOW BEFORE YOU ORDER

- **COPYRIGHT** These plans are protected under Copyright Law. Reproduction by any means is strictly prohibited. The right of building only one structure from these plans is licensed exclusively to the buyer and these plans may not be resold unless by express written authorization from home designer/architect. You may not use this design to build a second or multiple dwelling(s) without purchasing another blueprint or blueprints or paying additional design fees. Each violation of the Copyright Law is punishable in a fine.

- **EXCHANGE POLICIES** Since blueprints are printed in response to your order, we cannot honor requests for refunds. However, if for some reason you find that the plan you have purchased does not meet your requirements, you may exchange that plan for another plan in our collection. At the time of the exchange, you will be charged a processing fee of 25% of your original plan package price, plus the difference in price between the plan packages (if applicable) and the cost to ship the new plans to you.

- **BUILDING CODES & REQUIREMENTS** At the time the construction drawings were prepared, every effort was made to ensure that these plans and specifications meet nationally recognized codes. Our plans conform to most national building codes. Because building codes vary from area to area, some drawing modifications and/or the assistance of a professional designer or architect may be necessary to comply with your local codes or to accommodate specific building site conditions. We advise you to consult with your local building official for information regarding codes governing your area.

- **REPRODUCIBLE MASTERS** If you wish to make some minor design changes, you'll want to order reproducible masters. These drawings contain the same information as the blueprints but are printed on erasable and reproducible paper which clearly indicates your right to copy or reproduce. This will allow your builder or a local design professional to make the necessary drawing changes without the major expense of redrawing the plans. This package also allows you to print copies of the modified plans as needed. The right of building only one structure from these plans is licensed exclusively to the buyer. You may not use this design to build a second or multiple dwelling(s) without purchasing another blueprint. Each violation of the Copyright Law is punishable in a fine.

Please note: Reproducible drawings can only be exchanged if the package is unopened, and exchanges are allowed only within 90 days of purchase.

BLUEPRINT PRICE SCHEDULE

Price Code	1-Set	Additional Sets	Reproducible Masters
P4	$20.00	$10.00	$70.00
P5	$25.00	$10.00	$75.00
P6	$30.00	$10.00	$80.00
P7	$50.00	$10.00	$100.00
P8	$75.00	$10.00	$125.00
P9	$125.00	$20.00	$200.00
P10	$150.00	$20.00	$225.00
P11	$175.00	$20.00	$250.00
P12	$200.00	$20.00	$275.00
P13	$225.00	$45.00	$440.00

**Plan prices guaranteed through December 31, 2004.
Please note that plans are not refundable.**

SHIPPING & HANDLING CHARGES
EACH ADDITIONAL SET ADD $2.00 TO SHIPPING CHARGES

U.S. SHIPPING
Regular *(allow 7–10 business days)* $5.95
Priority *(allow 3–5 business days)* $15.00
Express* *(allow 1–2 business days)* $25.00

CANADA SHIPPING
Standard *(allow 8–12 business days)* $15.00
Express* *(allow 3–5 business days)* $40.00

OVERSEAS SHIPPING/INTERNATIONAL
Call, fax, or e-mail (plans@hdainc.com) for shipping costs.

* For express delivery please call us by 11:00 a.m. CST

How To Order

**For fastest service,
Call Toll-Free 1-800-367-7667 day or night**
Three Easy Ways To Order

1. CALL toll free 1-800-367-7667 for credit card orders. MasterCard, Visa, Discover and American Express are accepted.
2. FAX your order to 1-314-770-2226.
3. MAIL the Order Form to:

   **HDA, Inc.
   4390 Green Ash Drive
   St. Louis, MO 63045**

**QUESTIONS?
Call Our Customer Service Number
314-770-2228**

ORDER FORM

Please send me -
PLAN NUMBER PB7-_____
PRICE CODE_____ (see Plan Page)

Reproducible Masters (see chart at left) $_____
Initial Set of Plans $_____
Additional Plan Sets (see chart at left)
_____ (Qty) at $_____ each $_____
Material List $50 each
Only available for plan ordered (see list below)
☐ PB7-0241 ☐ PB7-0242 ☐ PB7-0243
☐ PB7-0461 ☐ PB7-0476 ☐ PB7-0658
☐ PB7-0700 ☐ PB7-N118
☐ PB7-N145 ☐ PB7-N147 $_____
Subtotal $_____
Sales Tax (MO residents add 6%) $_____
☐ Shipping / Handling (see chart at left) $_____
(each additional set add $2.00 to shipping charges)

TOTAL ENCLOSED (US funds only) $_____

☐ Enclosed is my check or money order payable to HDA, Inc. (Sorry, no COD's)

I hereby authorize HDA, Inc. to charge this purchase to my credit card account (check one):

☐ MasterCard ☐ VISA ☐ DISCOVER NOVUS ☐ AMERICAN EXPRESS Cards

Credit Card number _____
Expiration date _____
Signature _____
Name _____
(Please print or type)
Street Address _____
(Please **do not** use PO Box)
City _____
State _____ Zip _____
Daytime phone number (____) -_____

Thank you for your order!

Deluxe Cabana

Design #PB7-12020

- Size - 11'-0" wide x 13'-6" deep
- Height floor to peak - 11'-7"
- Ceiling height - 8'-0"
- Unique roof design with skylight
- Convenient dressing room
- Perfect storage for poolside furniture and equipment
- Concrete floor
- Includes complete list of materials
- Step-by-step instructions

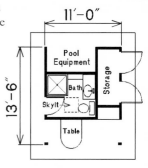

Price Code P6

Gable Storage Shed/Playhouse

Design #PB7-12024

- Size - 12' wide x 8' deep
- Height floor to peak - 10'-5"
- Ceiling height - 8'-0"
- 3'-0" x 6'-8" dutch door
- Perfect for storage or playhouse for children
- Shutters and window box create a charming facade
- Wood floor on 4x4 runners
- Includes complete list of materials
- Step-by-step instructions

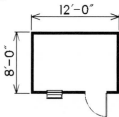

Price Code P5

Garden Shed

Design #PB7-12008

- Size - 12' wide x 10' deep
- Height floor to peak - 9'-9"
- Rear wall height - 7'-1 1/2"
- Features skylight windows for optimal plant growth
- Ample room for tool and lawn equipment storage
- Wood floor on gravel base
- Includes complete list of materials
- Step-by-step instructions

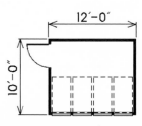

Price Code P5

Gable Storage Sheds

Design #PB7-12010

- Three popular sizes -
  8' wide x 8' deep
  8' wide x 10' deep
  8' wide x 12' deep
- Height floor to peak - 9'-1"
- Wall height - 6'-7"
- Circle-top window adds interest and light
- Wood floor on concrete footings
- Includes complete list of materials
- Step-by-step instructions

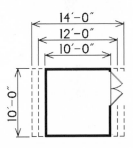

Price Code P5

Garden Sheds With Clerestory

Design #PB7-12017

- Three popular sizes -
  10' wide x 10' deep
  12' wide x 10' deep
  14' wide x 10' deep
- Height floor to peak - 10'-11"
- Rear wall height - 7'-3"
- 5'-0" x 6'-9" double-door
- Clerestory windows for added light
- Wood floor on 4x6 runners
- Includes complete list of materials
- Step-by-step instructions

Price Code P5

Children's Playhouse

Design #PB7-12019

- Size - 6' wide x 6' deep
- Height floor to peak - 7'-2"
- Wall height - 4'-4"
- Plenty of windows brighten interior
- Attractive Victorian style
- Gabled doorway and window box add interest
- Wood floor on gravel base
- Includes complete list of materials
- Step-by-step instructions

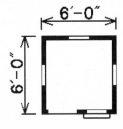

Price Code P4

Garden Shed

Design #PB7-12025

- Size - 10' wide x 10' deep
- Height floor to peak - 11'-3 1/2"
- Left wall height - 8'-0"
- Wonderful complement to any backyard
- Perfect space for lawn equipment or plants and flowers
- Plenty of windows for gardening year-round
- Wood floor on 4x4 runners
- Includes complete list of materials
- Step-by-step instructions

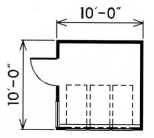

Price Code P5

Playhouse/Storage Shed

Design #PB7-12013

- Size - 8' wide x 12' deep
- Height floor to peak - 10'-6"
- Ceiling height - 7'-0"
- 3'-0" x 6'-0" door
- Quaint chalet design
- Ideal playhouse in summer
- Storage shed in the off season
- Wood floor on concrete piers or concrete floor
- Includes complete list of materials
- Step-by-step instructions

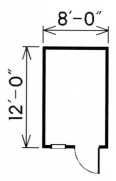

Price Code P4

Children's Playhouse

Design #PB7-12006

- Size - 8' wide x 8' deep
- Height floor to peak - 9'-2"
- Ceiling height - 6'-1"
- 2' deep porch
- Attractive window boxes
- Includes operable windows
- Wood floor on 4x4 runners
- Includes complete list of materials
- Step-by-step instructions

Price Code P4

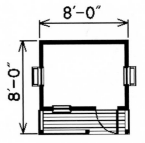

Convenience Shed

Design #PB7-12007

- Size - 16' wide x 12' deep
- Height floor to peak - 12'-4 1/2"
- Ceiling height - 8'-0"
- 8'-0" x 7'-0" overhead door
- Ideal for lawn equipment or small boat storage
- Oversized windows brighten interior
- Concrete floor
- Includes complete list of materials
- Step-by-step instructions

Price Code P6

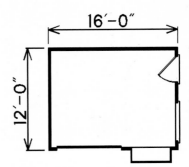

Workroom With Covered Porch

Design #PB7-15021

- Size - 24' x 20'
- Building height - 13'-6"
- Roof pitch - 6/12
- Ceiling height - 8'-0"
- Easy access through double-door entry
- Interior enhanced by large windows
- Large enough for storage
- Slab foundation
- Includes complete list of materials
- Step-by-step instructions

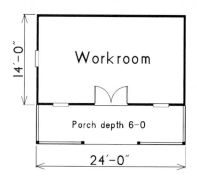

Price Code P8

Large Poolside Structure

Design #PB7-15024

- Size - 20' x 22'
- Building height - 13'-5"
- Roof pitch - 6/12
- Ceiling height - 8'-0"
- Two dressing areas both with shower and toilet
- Covered area ideal for snack/ drink bar
- Storage area accessible to outdoors for lawn and pool equipment
- Slab foundation
- Includes complete list of materials
- Step-by-step instructions

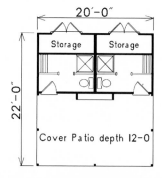

Price Code P7

Barn Storage Sheds With Loft

Design #PB7-12002

- Three popular sizes -
  12' wide x 12' deep
  12' wide x 16' deep
  12' wide x 20' deep
- Height floor to peak - 12'-10"
- Ceiling height - 7'-4"
- 4'-0" x 6'-8" double-door
- Wood floor on concrete pier foundation or concrete floor
- Includes complete list of materials
- Step-by-step instructions

Price Code P5

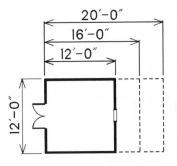

3-Seasons Room

325 total square feet of living area

Design #PB7-15005

- Building height - 13'-6"
- Roof pitch - 6/12
- Wall height - 8'-0"
- Perfect for entertaining
- Plenty of sunlight permits plants and flowers
- Includes complete list of materials
- Step-by-step instructions

Price Code P8

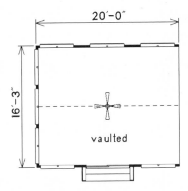

To order, use the form on page 127 or call 1-800-367-7667

Weekender Cottage
144 total square feet of living area

Price Code P6

- Building height -14'-6"
- Ceiling height - 10'-0"
- 2" x 6" exterior walls
- Roof pitch - 12/12 and 5/12
- Cottage could easily become a home office space or a guest house
- Multiple built-ins make storage simple
- Slab foundation
- Includes complete list of materials

12' (3.66m)
16' (4.88m)
built - in bunk beds
table space
verandah

Wooded Getaway
676 total square feet of living area

Price Code P13

Design #PB7-15502

- Building height - 17'-9"
- Roof pitch - 6/12
- Ceiling height - 8'-0"
- 1 bedroom, 1 bath
- Open floor plan features see-through fireplace and full-length porch
- Crawl space foundation
- Includes complete list of materials

26'-0"
26'-0"
Br 1
11-6x11-0
Kit
7-10x8-0
Living
14-2x14-0
Din
11-2x8-5
Covered Porch depth 6-0

Exclusive Retreat
480 total square feet of living area

Price Code P11

Design #PB7-15506

- Building height - 14'-2"
- Roof pitch - 6/12
- Ceiling height - 8'-0"
- 1 bedroom, 1 bath
- Cozy cabin includes large fireplace in sitting area with views into dining area
- Slab foundation
- Includes complete list of materials

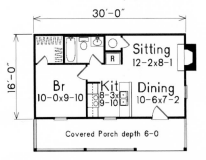

Studio Home Office
432 total square feet of living area

Price Code P8

Design #PB7-15512

- Building height - 19'-6"
- Roof pitch - 12/12
- Ceiling height - 9'-0"
- 2" x 6" exterior walls
- Studio/home office is flooded with sunlight from large windows
- French door accesses covered porch creating an outdoor living area
- Loft above bath allows for storage
- Crawl space or slab foundation, please specify when ordering
- Includes complete list of materials

Sport Cabin

576 total square feet of living area

Price Code P10

Design #PB7-15009

- Building height - 25'-6"
- Roof pitch - 6/12
- Ceiling height - 8'-0"
- 2 bedrooms, 1 bath
- Ideal for avid hunter or fisherman
- Pier foundation
- Includes complete list of materials
- Step-by-step instructions

24'-0"

24'-0"

Br 1
12-0x11-4

Br 2
11-1x8-4

Living
15-4x11-8

Kitchen
8-0x9-4

Porch depth 8-0

A-Frame Cottage

960 total square feet of living area

Price Code P10

Design #PB7-15014

- Building height - 22'-0"
- Roof pitch - 24/12
- 1 bedroom, 1 sleeping loft and 1 bath
- Open central living area is functional and spacious
- Plenty of storage throughout
- Pier foundation
- Includes complete list of materials
- Step-by-step instructions

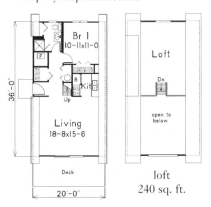

36'-0"

Br 1
10-11x11-0

Living
18-8x15-6

Deck

20'-0"

first floor
720 sq. ft.

Loft

Dn

open to below

loft
240 sq. ft.

Graciously Designed Refuge

527 total square feet of living area

Material List Available

Price Code P13

Design #PB7-N118

- Cleverly arranged home has it all
- Foyer spills into the dining nook with access to side views
- An excellent kitchen offers a long breakfast bar and borders the living room with free-standing fireplace
- A cozy bedroom has a full bath just across the hall
- 1 bedroom, 1 bath
- Crawl space foundation

Cottage-Style, Appealing And Cozy

828 total square feet of living area

Material List Available

Price Code P13

Design #PB7-0461

- Vaulted ceiling in living area enhances space
- Convenient laundry room
- Sloped ceiling creates unique style in bedroom #2
- Efficient storage space under the stairs
- Covered entry porch provides cozy sitting area and plenty of shade
- 2 bedrooms, 1 bath
- Crawl space foundation

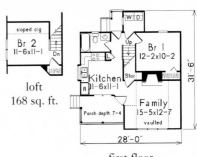

loft
168 sq. ft.

first floor
660 sq. ft.

A Cottage With Class
576 total square feet of living area

Material List Available

Price Code P13

Design #PB7-0476

- Perfect country retreat features vaulted living room and entry with skylights and plant shelf above
- Double-doors enter a vaulted bedroom with bath access
- Kitchen offers generous storage and pass-through breakfast bar
- 1 bedroom, 1 bath
- Crawl space foundation

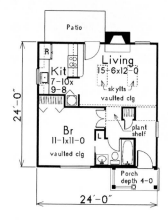

Double Dormers Accent This Cozy Vacation Retreat
581 total square feet of living area

Material List Available

Price Code P13

Design #PB7-0243

- Kitchen/living room features space for dining and spiral steps leading to the loft area
- Large loft space can easily be converted to a bedroom or work area
- Entry space has a unique built-in display niche
- 1 bedroom, 1 bath
- Slab foundation

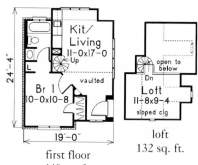

first floor
449 sq. ft.

loft
132 sq. ft.

To order, use the form on page 127 or call 1-800-367-7667

Large Front Porch Adds Welcoming Appeal

829 total square feet of living area

Material List Available

Price Code P13

Design #PB7-0241

- U-shaped kitchen opens into living area by a 42" high counter
- Oversized bay window and French door accent dining room
- Gathering space is created by the large living room
- Convenient utility room and linen closet
- 1 bedroom, 1 bath
- Slab foundation

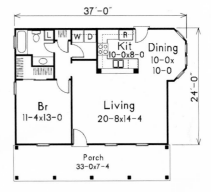

37'-0"

W D

Kit 10-0x8-0

Dining 10-0x 10-0

24'-0"

Br 11-4x13-0

Living 20-8x14-4

Porch 33-0x7-4

Year-Round Hideaway

416 total square feet of living area

Material List Available

Price Code P13

Design #PB7-0700

- Open floor plan creates spacious feeling
- Covered porch has rustic appeal
- Plenty of cabinetry and workspace in kitchen
- Large linen closet centrally located and close to bath
- Sleeping area, 1 bath
- Slab foundation

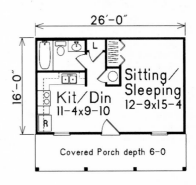

26'-0"

16'-0"

L

Sitting/ Sleeping 12-9x15-4

Kit/Din 11-4x9-10

Covered Porch depth 6-0

Sensational Cottage Retreat
647 total square feet of living area

Material List Available

Price Code P13

- Large vaulted room for living/sleeping with plant shelves on each end, stone fireplace and wide glass doors for views
- Roomy kitchen is vaulted and has a bayed dining area and fireplace
- Step down into a sunken and vaulted bath featuring a 6'-0" whirlpool tub-in-a-bay with shelves at each end for storage
- A large palladian window adorns each end of the cottage giving a cheery atmosphere throughout
- 1 living/sleeping room, 1 bath
- Crawl space foundation

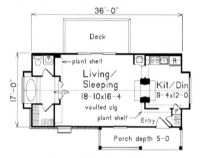

An A-Frame For Every Environment
618 total square feet of living area

Material List Available

Price Code P13

Design #PB7-N145

- Memorable family events are certain to be enjoyed on this fabulous partially covered sundeck
- Equally impressive is the living area with its cathedral ceiling and exposed rafters
- A kitchenette, bedroom and bath conclude the first floor with a delightful sleeping loft above bedroom and bath
- 1 bedroom, 1 bath
- Pier foundation

first floor
480 sq. ft.

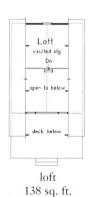

loft
138 sq. ft.

Recessed Stone Entry Provides A Unique Accent

717 total square feet of living area

Design #PB7-0242

- Incline ladder leads up to cozy loft area
- Living room features plenty of windows and vaulted ceiling
- U-shaped kitchen includes a small bay window at the sink
- 1 bedroom, 1 bath
- Slab foundation

Material List Available

Price Code P13

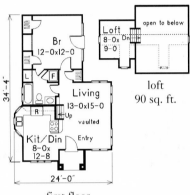

loft
90 sq. ft.

first floor
627 sq. ft.

Terrific Design Loaded With Extras

865 total square feet of living area

Design #PB7-N147

- Central living area provides an enormous amount of space for gathering around the fireplace
- Outdoor ladder on wrap-around deck connects top deck with main deck
- Kitchen is bright and cheerful with lots of windows and access to deck
- 2 bedrooms, 1 bath
- Pier foundation

Material List Available

Price Code P13

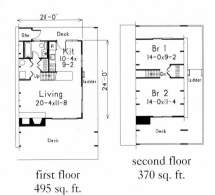

first floor
495 sq. ft.

second floor
370 sq. ft.

design and photography credits

design

FRONT MATTER

4 bottom Design: LeAnna Olson

PLANNING YOUR COTTAGE

6 Garden Design: Bob Dash **10** Design: Bob Dal Bon/Structure 1 **11 top** Landscape Design: James David **11 bottom left and right** Design: Barbara Butler Artist-Builder, Inc. **12 bottom** Architect: Carol A. Wilson **13 top** Architect: Charles M. Moore/Moore-Poe Architects; Construction: Charles Mize/ The Wilson-Mize Company **18** Architect: Barbara Chambers/ Chambers and Chambers; Construction: Dougall Construction **20 bottom** Design/Construction: Matt Erwin and Tamsen McCracken **22 bottom** Architect: Roc Caivano **23 top** Design/ Construction: Sam Eskildsen **23 bottom** Architect: George Israel for Southern Living Plans **25 top** Architect: Robert C. Chestnut for Southern Living Plans **25 bottom** Design: Amdega Limited **28 bottom** Design: Van-Martin Rowe Design of Pasadena **29 bottom** Design: Grant Liere and Nixie Barton **30 top** Design: Leonna Duff **31 top right** Decorative Painting: Pam Snell **31 bottom** Design: Sheri Sayre

A GALLERY OF COTTAGES

32 Architect: Lee H. Skolnick **34 bottom–35** Architect: David Trachtenberg/Trachtenberg Architects; Landscape Architect: Robert Trachtenberg/Garden Architecture; Contractor: Mueller Nicholls, Inc. **36–37 top** Design: Kim and Debie Stuart **37 bottom** Architect/Builder: Bill Galli; Landscape Designer: Peter Koenig **38** Interior Design: Michael D. Trapp **39** Design: Laura Courtney **40** Architect: Roc Caivano **41** Design: Tim Prentice **42 bottom** Design: Barbara and Gary Greensweig **43 top** Design: Ronald Lee Fleming/The Townscape Institute; Housewright: Tom Curtis **43 bottom** Design: Stephanie and Larry Feeney **44 bottom–45** Design: Robert and Nancy Tiner **47** Design: Janet Tiffany **48** Garden Design: Jacqueline Heriteau and Holly B. Hunter **49** Design: Penny Michels **50 bottom–51** Architect: Mark A. Hutker/Mark Hutker Associates & Architects Inc.; Landscape Architect: Steve Stimson/Stephen Stimson Associates **52** Architect: Charles Myer/Charles R. Myer & Co.; Builder: Michael Pollen **53** Architect: Tom Cullins/Truex Cullins & Partners Architects **54–55** Architect: Kathryn Rogers/Sogno Design Group **57** Design: Alicia and Bill Hitchcock **58 bottom–59** Design: Josef H. Maison/Custom Log, Ltd.; Interior Design: Nancy Maison/A Great Find **60 top** Design: Carol Anthony **60 bottom** Design: Diane Stevenson Design; Stonework: Michael Murphy; Leaded Glass: Alan Masaoka **61** Interior Design: Michael D. Trapp **62 bottom left** Design: Hap and Barbara Arnold **62 bottom right** Design: Sharon Fisher **63 top left** Design: Carol Biel **63 top right** Design: Brian and Debrah Nelson **63 bottom** Design: Barbara Butler Artist-Builder, Inc. **65** Design: David Phillips **66** Architect: Michael Keller **67** Courtyard Design: Carlos Mora; Garden Design: Yvonne Axene, assisted by Saul Velsquez **68–69 top** Design: Barbara Greensweig; Design/ Construction: Jim Tranchina **69 bottom** Design: Harriet Adams/The Potager **71** Architect: Mark A. Hutker/Mark Hutker Associates & Architects, Inc.; Landscape Architect: Steve Stimson/ Stephen Stimson Associates **72–73 all** Architect: McKee Patterson/Austin Patterson Disston Architects **74 bottom** Design: Gardensheds; Garden Design: Paula Mancester **75 top** Design: Charles de Lisle/The Charles de Lisle Program; Decorative Painting: Willem Racké/Willem Racké Studios **75 bottom** Design: Sweetwater Bungalows **76** Design: Hal Ainsworth for Southern Living Plans **77** Design: Amdega Limited; Interior Design: Vic and Carolyn Riches **79 top** Design: Ray Hugenberger, and Bob Dal Bon/Structure 1 **80 bottom–81** Architect: Roc Caivano **82–83** Design: Ene Osteraas-Constable/WOWHAUS, www.thewowhaus.com **84–85** Architect: Robert Remiker; Interior Design: Sarita Patel; Landscape Design: Angela and Tom Campbell **86–87** Architect: Rob Whitten **88–89** Architect: Jarvis Architects **90 bottom–91** Architect: Adrian Martinez; Construction: Doug Earl Construction and Marshall Vincent Construction; Interior Design: Ken and Noni Kahn and David Phillips; Garden Design: Geared for Growing **92** Architect: T. Scott Teas/TFH Architects **93 top** Architectural and Interior Design: Pamela Dreyfuss Interior Design; Millwork and Doors: Creative Cabinets **93 bottom** Courtyard Design: Carlos Mora; Garden Design: Yvonne Axene assisted by Saul Velsquez **94–95** Architect: Dennis O'Conner/The O'Conner Company; Landscape Architect: Marta Fry Landscape; Interior Design: Elizabeth Hill/Selby House **96 bottom** Design: Tim Prentice **97** Design/Construction: Jim Knott

COTTAGE ELEMENTS

98 Design: Laura Courtney; Chair Artist: Tim Whyard **100 top** Design: Elizabeth Lair Design **100 bottom** Design: Peter Wooster **101 top left** Architect: Scott Design Associates **101 top center** Architects: Richard Bernhard and John Priestly/ Bernhard & Priestly Architects; Builder: Jay Fischer/Cold Mountain Builders **102 bottom right** Garden Design: Bob Dash **103 bottom** Design: Linda Hoffman/Guided Imagery Productions **106 bottom right** Architects: Bill Curtis and Russell Windham/Curtis & Windham Architects; Builder: Temple Pace/ Pace Development, Inc. **107 bottom left** Design: Elaine Shreve **108 top** Courtyard Design: Carlos Mora; Garden

photography

If not otherwise credited, photographs are by **Jamie Hadley**.

Jean Allsopp: 69 bottom left and right, 106 bottom right; **Frank Balthis:** 75 bottom; **Karen Bussolini:** 5, 11 top, 49 all, 120 top and bottom center; **Brian Carter/The Garden Picture Library:** 107 bottom right; **Crandall & Crandall:** 120 top left; **Eric Crichton/The Garden Picture Library:** 104 top; **Robin Cushman:** 4 bottom; **Ken Druse:** 124 top right; **Derek Fell:** 26, 101 left center, 106 top; **Jay Graham:** 36, 37 top left and right; **Ken Gutmaker:** 37 bottom, 125 bottom; **Lynne Harrison:** 79 bottom right, 100 top, 101 top right, 102 bottom left, 107 top, 143; **Margot Hartford:** 120 top right; **Philip Harvey:** 16, 20 top, 28 bottom, 34 top, 57 all, 108 bottom left, 109 both, 112 bottom left, 123 top left and bottom right; **Douglas Johnson Photography:** 31 top right, 114 top right; **Muffy Kibbey:** 18; **Lamontagne/The Garden Picture Library:** 29 top; **David McDonald:** 43 bottom; **E. Andrew McKinney:** 3 third from bottom, 4 top, 10, 28 top, 34 bottom, 35 both, 44 bottom, 45 both, 77 both, 79 top and bottom left, 82, 83 both, 94, 95 both, 97 both, 99, 101 top left, 111 bottom right, 112 bottom right, 116 bottom, 117 bottom right, 119 top left and right, 120 bottom right, 122 top, 124 top

left; **Allan Mandell:** 29 bottom, 31 bottom, 101 bottom center, 107 bottom left, 118, 125 top left; **Charles Mann:** 60 top, 101 bottom right, 111 top right; **Sylvia Martin:** 23 top, 105 bottom right; **Stephanie Massey:** 9; **Steven Mays:** 115 top right; **Emily Minton:** 13 top, 76 both, 122 bottom left; **Terrence Moore:** 114 left; **Jerry Pavia:** 6, 13 bottom center and right, 14, 78 bottom, 102 left center and bottom right, 103 top, 105 top and center right, 106 bottom left, 116 top; **John Peden:** 52 both; **Robert Perron:** 70 bottom; **David Phelps:** 113 bottom right; **Norman A. Plate:** 103 bottom; **Susan A. Roth:** 30 top, 74 bottom, 110 both; **James R. Salomon:** 12 bottom; **Sibila Savage:** 66 both; **Michael Skott:** 1, 2, 102 top left, 105 center, 123 bottom left, 124 bottom, 125 top right; **Robin Stancliff:** 121 bottom left; **John Sutton:** 121 top; **Tim Street-Porter/www.beateworks. com:** 115 bottom; **Thomas J. Story:** 119 bottom; **Van Chaplin:** 23 bottom, 25 top; **Brian Vanden Brink:** 30 bottom, 31 top left, 86, 87 both, 112 top right; **David Wakely:** 121 bottom right, 122 bottom right; **Jessie Walker:** 8 bottom

Design: Yvonne Axene assisted by Saul Velsquez **109 top** Fireclay Tile **110 bottom** Design: Conni Cross **111 bottom center** Hadco Lighting **112 top right** Interior Design: Drysdale Associates Interior Design **112 bottom right** Interior Design: Elizabeth Hill/Selby House; Architect: Dennis O'Conner/The O'Conner Company **113 top left** Architect: Roc Caivano **113 bottom left** Interior Design: Pamela Dreyfuss Interior Design **113 center** Interior Design: Ken and Noni Kahn and David Phillips **113 top right** Architect: Roc Caivano **113 bottom right** Design: Georgie Kajer/Kajer Architects **114 left** Design: Brad Tito/Lazok Tito Consulting **114 right** Decorative Painting: Pam Snell **115 top left** Architect: Jarvis Architects **115 top right** Decorative Painting: Justina Jorrin Barnard **115 center** Architect: Mark A. Hutker/Mark Hutker Associates & Architects, Inc. **115 bottom** Design: Paul Zsafen **117 top right** Interior Design: Nancy Maison/A Great Find **118** Design: Sheri Sayre **119 top left** Design: Freddy Moran, and Carlene Anderson

Kitchen Design **119 top right** Design: Robert and Nancy Tiner **119 bottom** Design: Mary Jo Bowling **120 top left** Design: Barbara Baker **120 top right** Design: Dirk Stennick, Architect **120 top and bottom center** Design: Penny Michels **121 top** Design: Dan Phipps & Associates Architects; Cabinets: Detail A Studios **121 bottom left** Design: Mark Adolph/Creative Concepts Design & Construction, and Sandy Hogan **121 bottom right** Design: Carolyn and Russ Walker; Sink and Faucet: Kohler **122 top** Architect: Bassenian/ Lagoni Architects; Interior Design: Pacific Dimensions, Inc. **122 bottom left** Architect: Charles M. Moore/Moore-Poe Architects; Cabinetmaker: James Jennings **122 bottom right** Interior Design: Janice Stone for Sunset's California Idea House **123 top left** Interior Design: Kremer Design Group **123 top right** Architect: Mark A. Hutker/ Mark Hutker Associates & Architects, Inc. **123 bottom right** GardenHome **124 bottom** Interior Design: Roberta Brown Root **125 top left** Design: Claire and Jamie Wright

index

Numbers in **boldface type** refer to photographs or illustrations.